COOL
Rome

teNeues

Imprint

Editors: Martin Nicholas Kunz, Editorial coordination: Sandra-Mareike Kreß

Photos (location): photos Martin Nicholas Kunz, beside: © AlexanderPlatz JazzClub (AlexanderPlatz JazzClub), © Freni e Frizioni (Freni e Frizioni), © Martin Nicholas Kunz, Michelle Galindo (Antico Forno Roscioli, Casa Bleve, Crudo, Sant' Eustachio, Campo de' Fiori, Colosseum, Forum Romanum, Galleria Nazionale d'Arte Moderna, Museo d'Arte Contemporanea di Roma, Pantheon, Trastevere), © Massimo Aureli, Francesco Cafaro (Etabli), © Matteo Piazza (Il Palazzetto Wine Bar, La Perla), © Maud (Maud), © Maurizio Proietti (La Bottega del Cioccolato), © MET (MET), © Michelle Galindo (Il Pagliaccio, Azi, Libreria del Cinema, TAD, Vestiti Usati Cinzia, Volpetti, Pincio), © Mirta Lispi, Stefano Perrina (The Perfect Bun at Co2), © rHome (rHome), © Salotto 42 (Salotto 42), © Société Lutèce (Société Lutèce), © Somo (Somo), © Sora Lella (Sora Lella)

Cover photo (location): © rHome (rHome)

Back cover photos from top to bottom (location): © MET (MET), © Maud (Maud), © Michelle Galindo (TAD), © Martin Nicholas Kunz, Michelle Galindo (Campo de' Fiori)

Price categories: € = reasonable, €€ = moderate, €€€ = upscale, €€€€ = expensive

Introduction, texts: Bärbel Holzberg. Layout & Pre-press. Imaging: fusion publishing. Translations: Zoratti studio editoriale: Ingo Wagener (English), Rosa Enciso (French), Giulio Monteduro (Italian)

Produced by fusion publishing GmbH, Berlin www.fusion-publishing.com

Published by teNeues Publishing Group

teNeues Verlag GmbH + Co. KG
Am Selder 37
47906 Kempen, Germany
Tel.: 0049-(0)2152-916-0
Fax: 0049-(0)2152-916-111
E-mail: books@teneues.de

Press department:
arehn@teneues.de
Tel.: 0049-2152-916-202

www.teneues.com

teNeues Publishing Company
16 West 22nd Street
New York, NY 10010, USA
Tel.: 001-212-627-9090
Fax: 001-212-627-9511

teNeues Publishing UK Ltd.
York Villa, York Road
Byfleet
KT14 7HX, Great Britain
Tel.: 0044-1932-403509
Fax: 0044-1932-403514

teNeues France S.A.R.L.
93, rue Bannier
45000 Orléans, France
Tel.: 0033-2-38541071
Fax: 0033-2-38625340

ISBN: 978-3-8327-9236-7

RESTAURANTS & CAFÉS

CLUBS, LOUNGES & BARS

SHOPS

HIGHLIGHTS

SERVICE

Introduction

Rome is steeped in history. Each stone and each fragment has a story to tell from Rome's rise, heyday and fall. The abundance of art treasures and objects of interest from antiquity, the Renaissance and Baroque periods would be overwhelming if it were not for the Romans' nonchalance in dealing with their rich cultural heritage.

The eternal city's coolness factor was kept under close guard for a long time, but this changed drastically with the comprehensive renovation program for the millennium celebrations. Restoring the yellow ocher façades furnished Rome's long overlooked modern art with appropriate surroundings. The architect Odile Decq, for example, created a new and exciting environment for the MACRO set in a former brewery.

Young up-and-coming artists are discovering the city and its stylish shops, bars, clubs, and restaurants, which spring up like mushrooms and attract a cosmopolitan audience just like in New York or London.

Cool Rome will accompany you through the city's cultural highlights and hip places—to the Libreria del Cinema in Trastevere, where a cinema lover's paradise was created by a couple of friends, or to Monte Testaccio with its cool nightlife.

Still, traditions were created to be followed—something of special importance to the Roman way of life. On Sundays, people climb the Pincio with friends to enjoy the breathtaking view over the rooftops and the city's domes. And afterwards, they sit in the legendary Antico Caffè Greco, sipping a caffè—there is no such thing as an espresso in Italy.

Bärbel Holzberg

Einleitung

Rom atmet Geschichte. Jeder Stein, jedes Fragment erzählt von einem Ereignis – von Aufstieg, Prachtentfaltung und Niedergang. Die Fülle an Kunstschätzen und Sehenswürdigkeiten aus Antike, Renaissance und Barock ist überwältigend, wäre da nicht die Lässigkeit der Römer mit ihrem reichen kulturellen Erbe umzugehen.

Der Coolnessfaktor der Ewigen Stadt war lange eher unterentwickelt, was sich mit dem umfassenden Sanierungsprogramm zur Jahrtausendwende gründlich änderte. Mit der Restaurierung der ockergelben Fassaden bekam auch die lange vernachlässigte moderne Kunst einen angemessenen Rahmen. So schuf beispielsweise die Architektin Odile Decq für das MACRO ein aufsehenerregendes neues Quartier, dass an ein altes Brauereigebäude angeschlossen ist.

Junge, aufstrebende Künstler entdecken die Stadt, in der an jeder Ecke stylische Shops, Bars, Klubs und Restaurants, wie sie auch in New York oder London ein kosmopolitisches Publikum ansprechen, aus dem Boden schießen.

Cool Rome führt zu den kulturellen Highlights und den angesagtesten Adressen, zur Libreria del Cinema in Trastevere, wo Freunde ein Eldorado für Cineasten kreiert haben, oder zum Monte Testaccio mit seiner hippen Nightlifeszene.
Daneben pflegen die Bewohner der Stadt Traditionen sorgsam, was für das ganz spezielle römische Lebensgefühl mindestens genauso wichtig ist. Mit Freunden steigt man am Sonntag auf den Pincio, um den atemberaubenden Blick über die Dächer und Kuppeln zu genießen und anschließend im legendären Antico Caffè Greco einen Caffè zu trinken – keinen Espresso, den kennt man in Italien nicht.

Bärbel Holzberg

Introduction

Rome respire l'histoire. Chaque pierre, chaque recoin raconte l'ascension, la splendeur et la décadence de l'Empire Romain. L'abondance de trésors artistiques et de curiosités datant de l'Antiquité, de la Renaissance et de l'époque baroque est étonnante, et pourtant les Romains ne se laissent pas impressionner par leur riche héritage culturel.

Le facteur « coolness » de la ville éternelle est resté plutôt minime pendant longtemps, mais depuis le nouveau millénaire, la situation a radicalement changé grâce à de vastes mesures de réhabilitation. Avec la restauration des façades ocre jaune, l'art moderne longtemps délaissé a enfin obtenu un cadre à sa mesure. Ainsi, l'architecte Odile Decq a créé pour le MACRO une nouvelle annexe spectaculaire, qui côtoie directement les bâtiments d'une vieille brasserie.

Les jeunes artistes montants découvrent la ville où des boutiques design, des bars, des clubs et des restaurants poussent comme des champignons à chaque coin de rue, attirant un public cosmopolite comme à Londres ou à New York.

Cool Rome vous mène aux centres d'intérêt culturel et aux adresses les plus branchées, à la Libreria del Cinema au Trastevere, par exemple, où un groupe d'amis a créé l'eldorado des cinéastes, ou bien encore au Monte Testaccio, avec sa vie nocturne et ses bars branchés.
Les Romains entretiennent pourtant leurs traditions qui font, elles aussi, partie intégrante de leur art de vivre très typique. Le dimanche, on grimpe avec des amis au Pincio pour jouir d'une vue à couper le souffle sur les toits et les coupoles de la ville, avant de se rendre au légendaire Antico Caffè Greco pour y boire un « caffè » – et non un « espresso », inconnu en Italie.

Bärbel Holzberg

Introducción

A Roma la storia si respira. Ogni pietra, ogni frammento racconta un'epoca: l'ascesa, i fasti, il declino. L'abbondanza di opere d'arte e di attrazioni risalenti all'antichità, al rinascimento e al barocco è straordinaria; a queste si contrappone la disinvoltura con cui i romani vivono il proprio ricco patrimonio culturale.

Il lato trendy della Città Eterna, a lungo ignorato, è potuto emergere grazie al programma di ristrutturazioni in occasione del passaggio al nuovo millennio. Con il restauro delle facciate giallo ocra anche l'arte moderna, a lungo trascurata, ha trovato una cornice adeguata. Così, ad esempio, l'architetto Odile Decq ha realizzato per il MACRO un nuovo sensazionale quartiere collegato a una vecchia fabbrica di birra.

Artisti giovani e ambiziosi scoprono una città nella quale in ogni angolo spuntano negozi, bar, club e ristoranti trendy, che, proprio come a Londra o a New York, si rivolgono a un pubblico cosmopolita.

Cool Rome guida il lettore attraverso i luoghi della cultura e quelli più alla moda, ad esempio alla Libreria del Cinema a Trastevere, dove un gruppo di amici ha creato l'eldorado dei cineasti, oppure a Monte Testaccio con la sua vita notturna di tendenza.
Allo stesso tempo gli abitanti della città curano attentamente anche le proprie tradizioni, senza le quali non sarebbe possibile garantire quella particolare gioia di vivere così tipicamente romana. La domenica si sale con gli amici sul Pincio per ammirare le viste spettacolari sui tetti e sulle cupole della città e poi bersi un caffè al leggendario Antico Caffè Greco.

Bärbel Holzberg

RESTAURANTS & CAFÉS

Antico Caffè Greco

Via dei Condotti, 86
00187 Rome
Centro Storico
Phone: +39 / 06 / 6 79 17 00
www.caffegreco.eu

Opening hours: Daily 9 am to 7.30 pm
Prices: €€€
Public transportation: Metro Piazza di Spagna
Map: No. 1

The stylish shops and fashion labels along the elegant Via Condotti may change, but the Caffè Greco stands above all that and remains what it was even in the times of Shelley and Byron. It is an absolute must for all visitors to Rome and a shelter of continuity. Already Casanova and Franz Liszt drank their coffee on the tiny marble tables and the walls were as bright red then as they are now.

Mögen die Edelläden der großen Modemarken auf der eleganten Via Condotti wechseln, das Caffè Greco bleibt, was es schon zu Goethes Zeiten war: ein absolutes Muss für alle Rombesucher und ein Hort der Beständigkeit. Schon Casanova und Franz Liszt tranken an den winzigen Marmortischen ihren Kaffee, und die Wände leuchteten damals genauso kräftig rot wie heute.

Si les enseignes des boutiques de luxe de l'élégante Via Condotti changent au fil du temps, le Caffè Greco, lui, reste ce qu'il était déjà du temps de Goethe: un endroit à ne pas manquer, un havre de continuité. Casanova et Franz Liszt déjà sirotaient leur café devant les minuscules tables de marbre et les murs ont gardé la teinte rouge vif de jadis.

Le boutique delle grandi griffe della moda lungo via Condotti potranno cambiare, ma il Caffè Greco rimane ciò che era già ai tempi di Goethe: un must per tutti i visitatori di Roma e una garanzia di inalterabilità. Già Casanova e Franz Liszt prendevano il caffè sui piccoli tavolini in marmo e le pareti brillavano allora dello stesso rosso acceso.

Antico Forno Roscioli

Via dei Giubbonari, 21
00186 Rome
Centro Storico
Phone: +39 / 06 / 6 87 52 87
www.anticofornoroscioli.com

Opening hours: Mon–Sat 12.30 pm to 4 pm and 6 pm to midnight
Prices: €€
Cuisine: Italian
Public transportation: Tramway Argentina
Map: No. 2

Russell James' Special Tip

This popular pizza shop's best pie is the bianca—a crispy, focaccia-like pizza painted with herbs and olive oil.

A long glass counter with delicious ham, sausages and cheese obtained directly from carefully selected producers will have you licking your chops as soon as you step into the restaurant. Quality and freshness are a hallmark of the eatery not far from the Campo de' Fiori. For example, they only use freshly caught fish from Civitavecchia or Anzio.

Eine lange Glastheke mit köstlichen Schinken, Würsten und Käsesorten, die direkt von sorgsam ausgewählten Produzenten bezogen werden, lässt einem schon beim Betreten das Wasser im Munde zusammenlaufen. Qualität und Frische der Produkte sind die Markenzeichen des Restaurants nicht weit vom Campo de' Fiori. So wird zum Beispiel ausschließlich fangfrischer Fisch aus Civitavecchia oder Anzio verarbeitet.

Dès que l'on pénètre dans ce restaurant, on a l'eau à la bouche à la vue seule du long bar en verre, garni de délicieux jambons, de charcuteries et de fromages appétissants, tous fournis par des producteurs soigneusement sélectionnés. La qualité et la fraîcheur des produits sont l'image de marque de ce local situé à proximité du Campo de' Fiori. Par exemple, on n'y sert que du poisson fraîchement pêché à Civitavecchia ou Anzio.

Una lunga vetrina con appetitose varietà di prosciutti, salsicce e formaggi, forniti direttamente da produttori selezionati, fa venire l'acquolina in bocca appena entrati. Qualità e prodotti freschi caratterizzano questo ristorante situato poco distante da Campo de' Fiori; il pesce servito qui, ad esempio, è stato appena pescato a Civitavecchia o ad Anzio.

Caffè della Pace

Via della Pace, 3/7
00186 Rome
Centro Storico
Phone: +39 / 06 / 6 86 12 16
www.caffedellapace.it

Opening hours: Daily 9 am to 3 am
Prices: €€
Public transportation: Bus to Chiesa Nuova
Map: No. 3

One of Rome's Dolce Vita hot spots. Few places have preserved the glamour of the '50s as well as the Caffè della Pace near the Piazza Navona. Luscious flower arrangements, red velvet sofas and mirrors with gold frames create an atmosphere that attracts VIPs from film and politics to this day. For celebrity sightings, gladly sip one of the Eternal City's most expensive cappuccinos.

Einer der Dolce-Vita-Hotspots Roms. An wenigen Orten hat sich der Glamour der 50er-Jahre so konserviert wie im Caffè della Pace nahe der Piazza Navona. Üppige Blumenarrangements, rote Samtsofas und goldgerahmte Spiegel schaffen eine Atmosphäre, die berühmte Persönlichkeiten aus Film und Politik bis heute anzieht. Für das Promigucken nimmt man gerne in Kauf, einen der teuersten Cappuccino der Ewigen Stadt zu trinken.

L'un des endroits chauds pour vivre la dolce vita à Rome. Les endroits sont peu nombreux à avoir conservé, comme lui le glamour des années cinquante. Les arrangements floraux exubérants du Caffè della Pace près de la Piazza Navona, ses fauteuils de velours rouge et ses miroirs aux cadres dorés attirent encore et toujours les personnalités du cinéma et de la politique. Pour entrevoir une célébrité, on ne recule pas devant le prix : le cappuccino est l'un des plus chers de la ville éternelle.

Una delle mete più gettonate della dolce vita romana. In pochi posti il glamour degli anni Cinquanta si è conservato così bene come al Caffè della Pace nei pressi di Piazza Navona. Rigogliose composizioni floreali, divanetti in velluto rosso e specchi con cornici dorate creano un'atmosfera che attira ancora oggi i personaggi dal mondo dello spettacolo e della politica. Per poter vedere i vip si accetta di buon grado di bere uno dei cappuccini più cari della Capitale.

Casa Bleve

Via del Teatro Valle 48/49
00186 Rome
Centro Storico
Phone: +39 / 06 / 6 86 59 70
www.casableve.it

Opening hours: Tue–Sat 12.30 am to 3 pm and 7.30 pm to 10.30 pm
Prices: €€€
Cuisine: Italian, only cold meals
Public transportation: Bus Rinascimento
Map: No. 4

Following the move from the Jewish quarter to the Centro Storico, the enoteca resides in an elegant mansion with columns and beautiful arches. The wine cellar harbors foundations from the time of Emperor Augustus. Mamma Tina continues to create delicious tidbits such as baked zucchini flowers or filled prosciutto rolls for the cold buffet which go perfectly with the wine on offer.

Nach dem Umzug aus dem jüdischen Viertel in das Centro Storico residiert die Enoteca in einem eleganten Stadtpalais mit Säulen und schön geschwungenen Bögen. Im Weinkeller finden sich noch Mauerreste aus der Zeit des Kaisers Augustus. Nach wie vor bereitet Mamma Tina die Köstlichkeiten für das kalte Buffet zu, wie gebackene Zucchiniblüten oder gefüllte Prosciutto-Röllchen, die perfekt mit den ausgeschenkten Weinen harmonieren.

Après avoir déménagé du quartier juif au Centro Storico, l'enoteca réside désormais dans un élégant palais urbain muni de colonnes et d'arcs élégants. À la cave se trouvent encore les vestiges de murs datant du temps de l'empereur Auguste. Comme toujours, Mamma Tina prépare les mets délicieux qui garnissent le buffet froid, tels que les beignets de fleur de courgette ou les petits rouleaux de prosciutto, qui s'harmonisent parfaitement avec le vin servi.

Dopo il trasloco dal ghetto ebraico nel centro storico, l'enoteca ha sede in un elegante palazzo con colonne e archi slanciati. Nella cantina si vedono ancora resti di muri risalenti all'era dell'imperatore Augusto. Come prima, mamma Tina prepara le prelibatezze per il buffet freddo, come i fiori di zucca fritti o i rotolini di prosciutto ripieni, perfettamente abbinati ai vini.

Crudo

Via degli Specchi, 6
00186 Rome
Centro Storico
Phone: +39 / 06 / 6 83 89 89
Site: www.crudoroma.it

Opening hours: Lunch daily noon to 3 pm, aperitif-dinner and American bar 7 pm to 2 am
Prices: €
Cuisine: International and fusion
Public transportation: Tram Argentina
Map: No. 5

Eva Padberg's Special Tip

This elegant eatery specializes in raw cuisine ranging from veal carpaccio to sashimi, complemented by flawless desserts.

Crudo, as the name suggests, is Rome's only raw foods restaurant and displays the coolness of a New York downtown lounge in a small alleyway near the Campo de' Fiori. Red leather armchairs and images projected on walls underline the cool vibe. "Drinking, eating, talking" is the name of the game and in that order at best—this place serves the ultimate vodka martini.

Crudo ist, wie der Name verspricht, das einzige Rohkostrestaurant Roms und hat die Coolness einer New Yorker Downtown-Lounge. Und das in einer kleinen Seitenstraße nahe dem Campo de' Fiori. Rote Ledersessel und an die Wände projizierte Bilder unterstreichen den coolen Vibe. „Trinken, essen, reden" lautet das Motto. Am besten, man hält sich an die Reihenfolge – bekommt man hier doch den perfekten Wodka Martini gemixt

Crudo est, comme son nom l'indique, le seul restaurant de crudités de Rome. Il a la classe d'un bar du centre ville new-yorkais. Et ceci malgré sa situation dans une petite rue latérale, près du Campo de' Fiori. Les fauteuils de cuir rouge et la projection de diapositives sur les murs soulignent son côté cool. « Boire, manger, parler », telle est la devise. Le mieux est de suivre l'ordre chronologique et de commencer par un Martini Vodka – c'est ici qu'il atteint la perfection.

Crudo, come dice il nome, è l'unico ristorante di specialità crude a Roma. Qui, in una stradina laterale nei pressi di Campo de' Fiori, troviamo lo stile sofisticato di una lounge degna di downtown Manhattan. Poltroncine in pelle rossa e immagini proiettate sulle pareti sottolineano l'atmosfera trendy. "Bere mangiare parlare", così recita il motto del ristorante. Si consiglia di seguire quest'ordine, cominciando dal Wodka Martini a regola d'arte.

Etablì

Vicolo delle Vacche, 9/9a
00186 Rome
Centro Storico
Phone: +39 / 06 / 97 61 66 94
www.etabli.it

Opening hours: Lunch noon to 3 pm, dinner 7 pm to midnight, winebar 6 pm to 2 am,
Mon closed
Prices: €€
Cuisine: Mediterranean
Public transportation: Bus to Chiesa Nuova
Map: No. 6

With Etablì, a curious mix between a wine bar, café and restaurant, the brothers Massimo and Alessandro Aurelio bring French shabby-chic to the River Tiber. Almost all furnishings stem from Southern France. The rustic Provençal workbenches gave the restaurant its name. One almost feels at home, sitting in leather armchairs around the open fire and chatting with friends.

Mit ihrem Etablì, das Weinbar, Café und Restaurant zugleich ist, bringen die Brüder Massimo und Alessandro Aurelio französischen Shabby-Chic an den Tiber. Fast die gesamte Einrichtung stammt aus Südfrankreich. Die rustikalen provenzalischen Werkbänke gaben dem Restaurant den Namen. Man kann sich ein wenig wie bei Freunden fühlen, auf Ledersesseln rund um den offenen Kamin sitzen und reden.

Avec l'Etablì, à la fois bar à vins, café et restaurant, les frères Massimo et Alessandro Aurelio apportent près du Tibre une note française de chic négligé. Presque tout le mobilier provient du sud de la France. Ce sont les établis provençaux rustiques qui ont donné son nom au restaurant. On s'y sent un peu comme chez des amis, à discuter dans des fauteuils en cuir autour de la cheminée.

Con il loro Etablì, che è contemporaneamente enoteca, caffè e ristorante, i fratelli Massimo e Alessandro Aurelio portano sul Tevere lo shabby chic francese. Quasi tutto l'arredamento proviene dal Sud della Francia. I banchi rustici dalla Provenza hanno dato il nome al ristorante. Qui ci si sente un po' come tra amici, parlando e sedendo sulle poltroncine in pelle intorno al caminetto aperto.

Giolitti al Vicario

Via Uffici del Vicario, 40
00186 Rome
Centro Storico
Phone +39 / 06 / 6 99 12 43
www.giolitti.it and www.giolitti.com

Opening hours: Daily 7 am to 2 am
Prices: €€
Public transportation: Metro to Barberini
Map: No. 7

Rome and ice cream, that is like an organic bond. It is simply unimaginable to start a summer evening in Rome without a sundae. The lines in front of the city's most famous and venerable gelateria are accordingly long. It is best to walk straight in and enjoy the house's main specialty, the Cassata Siciliana, in the beautifully conserved fin de siècle interior.

Rom und Eiscreme, das ist wie eine organische Verbindung. Unvorstellbar, in eine römische Sommernacht ohne Eisbecher zu starten. Entsprechend lang sind die Schlangen, die sich allabendlich vor Roms berühmtester und traditionsreichster Gelateria bilden. Am besten begibt man sich gleich nach drinnen und genießt im wundervoll erhaltenen Fin-de-Siècle-Interieur die Hausspezialität Cassata Siciliana.

Peut-on imaginer Rome sans ses « gelati » ? Impensable en effet de ne pas commencer une soirée estivale par une bonne coupe de glace. Ce qui explique les longues queues qui se forment chaque soir devant la gelateria la plus célèbre et la plus traditionnelle de Rome. Le mieux est de se rendre directement à l'intérieur pour y savourer une cassata siciliana, la spécialité de la maison, dans une merveilleuse ambiance fin de siècle.

Roma e i gelati: un vero connubio organico. Non si può cominciare una notte estiva romana senza una coppetta di gelato. Altrettanto lunghe sono la code che ogni sera si formano davanti alla gelateria più famosa e tradizionale di tutta Roma. Meglio recarsi subito all'interno e gustare, negli interni fin de siècle perfettamente conservati, la specialità della casa: la cassata siciliana.

Gusto

Piazza Augusto Imperatore, 9
00186 Rome
Centro Storico
Phone: +39 / 06 / 3 22 62 73
www.gusto.it

Opening hours: Daily 12.45 pm to 3 pm and 7.45 pm to midnight
Prices: €€
Cuisine: Italian
Public transportation: Bus to Lungotevere Augusta / Ara Pacis
Map: No. 8

It is loud and busy and simply cannot decide whether it should be a pizzeria, wine bar, restaurant, cookbook, or kitchen accessories shop, and is enormously popular. Gusto near the Mausoleum is an institution. It stands for uncomplicated food and the waiter will not express his or her displeasure if you order a simple pasta dish or a pizza. Wines are served by the glass.

Es ist laut, es ist umtriebig, kann sich nicht entscheiden, ob es Pizzeria, Weinbar, Restaurant, Kochbuchladen oder Geschäft für Küchenutensilien sein will – und es ist ungeheuer beliebt. Gusto am Mausoleum des Augustus ist eine Institution. Es steht für einen Trend, dass Essen unkompliziert sein kann und man nicht den Unmut des Kellners erregt, wenn man lediglich einen Teller Pasta oder eine Pizza ordert. Die Weine werden glasweise ausgeschenkt.

Bruyant et dynamique, cet endroit ne sait pas décider s'il est une pizzeria, un bar à vins, un restaurant, un magasin de livres de recettes ou d'ustensiles de cuisine – et il est extrêmement populaire. Le Gusto, près du Mausolée d'Auguste, est une institution. Ici la simplicité est de mise : le repas ne doit pas être forcément compliqué et on ne s'attirera pas les foudres du garçon en ne commandant qu'une assiette de pâtes ou une pizza. Les vins sont servis au verre.

È rumoroso, confusionario e non sa decidersi tra essere una pizzeria, un'enoteca, un ristorante, una libreria di manuali di culinaria o un negozio di utensili di cucina; eppure è incredibilmente amato. Gusto, nei pressi del mausoleo di Augusto, è un'istituzione, la dimostrazione che mangiare può essere una cosa facile e che è possibile ordinare solamente un piatto di pasta o una pizza senza scatenare il risentimento del cameriere. I vini vengono serviti a bicchieri.

Il Pagliaccio

Via dei Banchi Vecchi, 129 a
00186 Rome
Centro Storico
Phone: +39 / 06 / 68 80 95 95
www.ristoranteilpagliaccio.it

Opening hours: Mon–Tue 8 pm to 10.30 pm, Wed–Sat 12.30 pm to 2 pm and 8 pm
to 10.30 pm
Prices: €€€
Cuisine: Fusion
Public transportation: Bus to Corso Vittorio Emanuele / Tassoni
Map: No. 9

An eatery for connoisseurs that celebrates owner Anthony Genovese's creative Italian cuisine com-
plimented by Far Eastern touches. After working in Tokyo, Malaysia and Ravello, where he acquired
two Michelin stars, the top chef started his own fine restaurant in an 18th-century Roman townhouse.
Alsatian pâtissier Marion Lichtle creates true marvels when it comes to baked goods.

Ein Feinschmeckerlokal, in dem Besitzer Anthony Genovese eine kreative italienische Küche zelebriert,
die fernöstliche Einflüsse aufnimmt. Nach Stationen in Tokio, Malaysia und Ravello, wo er sich zwei
Michelin-Sterne erwarb, eröffnete der Spitzenkoch in einem feinen römischen Stadthaus aus dem
18. Jahrhundert sein eigenes Restaurant. Unterstützt wird er von der Elsässerin Marion Lichtle, die als
Patissier wahre Wunderwerke schafft.

Un restaurant pour les gourmets, dont le propriétaire Anthony Genovese célèbre une cuisine italienne
créative aux influences d'Extrême-Orient. Après avoir fait étape à Tokyo, en Malaisie et à Ravello, où il
a obtenu deux étoiles au Michelin, ce grand chef a ouvert son propre restaurant dans une villa romaine
du XVIIIe siècle. La pâtissière alsacienne Marion Lichtle lui prête main forte en créant de véritables
œuvres d'art.

Un locale per buongustai in cui il proprietario, Anthony Genovese, celebra una cucina italiana creativa
arricchita da influssi del lontano Oriente. Dopo le tappe a Tokyo, in Malaysia e a Ravello, dove si è
guadagnato due stelle Michelin, il celebre chef ha aperto un ristorante tutto suo in un raffinato palazzo
romano del XVIII secolo. Viene aiutato dalla pasticcera alsaziana Marion Lichtle che realizza veri e
propri capolavori di dolcezza.

MaterMatuta

Via Milano, 47
00187 Rome
Centro Storico
Phone: +39 / 06 / 47 82 57 46
www.matermatuta.net

Opening hours: Daily 12.30 pm to 3.30 pm and 7 pm to 12 am
Prices: €€
Cuisine: Mediterranean
Public transportation: Metro Cavour / Repubblica / Termini
Maps: No. 10

Wine and art combine perfectly in this restaurant in the Centro Storico. It is preferred by the locals who appreciate some 500 different wines on offer. The modern Italian interior kept in white, red and black provides a delightful contrast to the historical surroundings, which are home to constantly changing art exhibitions.

Wein und Kunst gehen in diesem Restaurant im Centro Storico, das bevorzugt von Einheimischen besucht wird, eine besonders glückliche Verbindung ein. 500 unterschiedliche Weine werden angeboten. Die moderne italienische Inneneinrichtung in Weiß, Rot und Schwarz bietet einen reizvollen Kontrast zu den historischen Räumen, in denen wechselnde Kunstausstellungen stattfinden.

Dans ce restaurant situé en plein centre historique et fréquenté surtout par les autochtones, le vin et l'art forment un mariage particulièrement heureux. On y propose 500 vins différents. L'aménagement moderne de style italien, en blanc, rouge et noir, crée un contraste intéressant avec les salles historiques, où se succèdent les expositions d'art.

Vino e arte creano un connubio particolarmente felice in questo ristorante del centro storico, frequentato di preferenza da avventori locali. Il MaterMatuta offre ben 500 vini diversi. Gli interni bianchi, rossi e neri, in stile italiano moderno, offrono un magnifico contrasto con gli spazi storici in cui vengono ospitate mostre d'arte a rotazione.

MET

Piazzale di Ponte Milvio, 34
00191 Rome
Ponte Milvio
Phone: +39 / 06 / 33 22 12 37
www.met-roma.it

Opening hours: Kitchen opens at 7.30 pm to 00.30 am, Mon closed
Price: €€
Cuisine: Italian Mediterranean
Public transportation: Tramway Pinturicchio
Map: No. 11

Russell James' Special Tip
Bright, airy and breezy, this trendy restaurant serves pizza, light Mediterranean fare and expertly curated wines.

Spacious rooms suffused with light and a large wooden terrace mark the MET. It is located somewhat away from the masses near the Ponte Milvio—an increasingly interesting area when it comes to food. On offer is a mix of sushi, light contemporary Italian cuisine, and excellent pizzas. In short: a mixture appreciated by city folk.

Große lichtdurchflutete Räume und eine weitläufige Holzterrasse zeichnen das MET aus, das etwas abseits der Touristenströme an der Ponte Milvio liegt – eine Gegend, die gastronomisch gerade interessant wird. Angeboten wird ein Mix aus Sushi, einer zeitgemäß leichten italienischen Küche und Pizzen von bester handwerklicher Qualität. Kurzum: eine Mischung, die Großstadtmenschen schätzen.

De grandes salles inondées de lumière et une vaste terrasse en bois caractérisent le MET, situé à deux pas du Ponte Milvio, un peu à l'écart des itinéraires touristiques, et dans un quartier qui commence à être connu pour sa gastronomie. On y sert une cuisine hétéroclite : sushis, cuisine italienne, moderne et légère, pizzas artisanales d'excellente qualité. Un mélange très apprécié des citadins !

Il MET è caratterizzato da ampie sale inondate di luce e da un'ampia terrazza in legno. Questo locale sorge presso il Ponte Milvio, un po' fuori dai flussi turistici, in una zona che sta diventando interessante dal punto di vista gastronomico. Qui viene proposto un mix di sushi, di cucina italiana contemporanea e di pizza artigianale della miglior qualità. In altre parole, una varietà apprezzata dagli abitanti di una metropoli.

The Perfect Bun at Co2

Largo del Teatro Valle, 4
00186 Rome
Centro Storico
Phone: +39 / 06 / 45 47 63 37
www.co2restaurant.it

Opening hours: Mon–Sat 6 pm to 2 am, Sun 12.45 pm to 3.30 pm
Prices: €€
Cuisine: American
Public transportation: Bus to Rinascimento
Map: No. 12

An innovative restaurant with a relaxed atmosphere in Sant'Eustachio, one of Rome's oldest districts. Prepare to get involved in a chat or two while sitting at the long tables and eating one of the many burgers, brownies, etc. available. Those complaining about small breakfasts should not miss Sunday brunch. Comfortable leather chairs invite you to relax in the evening.

Ein innovatives Restaurant mit relaxter Atmosphäre in Sant'Eustachio, einem der ältesten Stadtbezirke Roms. Es ist äußerst kommunikativ mittags an der langen Tafel zu sitzen und sich an dem breiten Angebot an Burgern, Brownies & Co. zu bedienen. Wer auf seiner Reise üppiges Frühstück vermisst, sollte sich das sonntägliche Brunch nicht entgehen lassen. Abends laden komfortable Ledersessel zur Entspannung ein.

Un restaurant innovateur et décontracté à Sant'Eustachio, l'un des arrondissements les plus anciens de Rome. Une ambiance très conviviale règne à midi autour de la longue table. On peut choisir parmi le riche assortiment de hamburgers, brownies etc. Les amateurs de petits déjeuners copieux ne devraient pas manquer le brunch dominical. Le soir, de confortables fauteuils en cuir invitent à la détente.

Un ristorante innovativo con un'atmosfera rilassata a Sant'Eustachio, uno dei più antichi quartieri di Roma. Sedere a mezzogiorno alla lunga tavola e servirsi dell'ampia scelta di burger, brownies e simili è estremamente comunicativo. Chi ama dilungarsi a colazione non dovrebbe perdersi il brunch domenicale. Di sera comode poltroncine in pelle invitano al relax.

rHome

Piazza Augusto Imperatore, 42
00186 Rom
Centro Storico
Phone: +39 / 06 / 68 30 14 30
www.ristoranterhome.com

Opening hours: Daily noon to 2.30 am, Sat closed at lunchtime
Prices: €€€
Cuisine: Italian
Public transportation: Metro Piazza di Spagna
Map: No. 13

The amount of Porsches and Ferraris hints at what is happening inside the restaurant. Ladies, prefer-ably clad in Roberto Cavalli creations and donning Dolce & Gabbana purses, and their perfectly tanned male counterparts clad in the finest cashmere have made this restaurant their home in Rome—as suggested by the name. Chrome, black marble and upholstered furniture by Poltrona Frau mark the interior.

Die Porsche- und Ferrari-Dichte im Umfeld des Restaurants sagt viel darüber aus, was sich im Innern abspielt. Die Damen der Gesellschaft, bevorzugt in Roberto Cavalli gewandet, mit Handtaschen von Dolce & Gabbana und braun gebrannte Männer in feinstem Kaschmir haben das Restaurant zu ihrem „Home" in Rom gemacht – nichts anderes meint der Name. Viel Chrome, schwarzer Marmor und Polstermöbel von Poltrona Frau bestimmen das Interieur.

Les Porsche et les Ferrari garées aux alentours du restaurant laissent deviner ce qui se passe à l'in-térieur. Les dames de la société, en Roberto Cavalli de préférence, sac à main Dolce & Gabbana au bras, et les hommes bronzés vêtus du cachemire le plus fin, ont élu domicile dans ce restaurant – d'où son nom. Une profusion de chrome, de marbre noir et de fauteuils de Poltrona Frau caractérisent l'intérieur.

La densità di Porsche e Ferrari intorno al ristorante è uno specchio fedele di ciò che vi si vede all'in-terno. Donne dell'alta società, preferibilmente avvolte in abiti firmati da Roberto Cavalli e con borsette Dolce & Gabbana, e uomini abbronzati in completi di cashmere hanno fatto del ristorante la propria "Home" a Roma, a cui allude il nome. Gli interni sono caratterizzati dall'abbondanza di cromo, di marmo nero e dai mobili imbottiti di Poltrona Frau.

SOMO

Via Goffredo Mameli, 5
00153 Rome
Trastevere
Phone: +39 / 06 / 5 88 20 60
www.somo.asia

Opening hours: Kitchen opens 7.30 pm to 00.30 am, Mon closed
Prices: €€
Cuisine: Japanese and fusion
Public transportation: Tramway Trastevere / Mastai
Map: No. 14

Eva Padberg's Special Tip
For a pasta break, try this sophisticated Japanese-fusion eatery's first-rate sushi and elegant cocktails.

Japanese esthetics meet Italian design in this stylish Asian restaurant. The fact that SOMO is located in the busy Trastevere district makes it only more interesting. The focus lies on Japanese cuisine with raw fish of the finest quality. It has a new take-out service and a shop with Japanese clothing and home accessories is in the works.

Japanische Ästhetik trifft italienisches Design in diesem stylischen asiatischen Restaurant. Dass das SOMO ausgerechnet im quirligen Trastevere beheimatet ist, macht den Kontrast besonders reizvoll. Der Schwerpunkt liegt auf japanischer Küche mit der Verarbeitung von rohem Fisch bester Qualität. Neuerdings gibt es ein Take-away; geplant ist die Eröffnung eines Shops mit japanischer Kleidung und Wohnaccessoires.

Dans ce restaurant asiatique, l'esthétique japonaise rencontre le design italien. Et que le SOMO soit situé dans le quartier pittoresque du Trastevere rend le contraste particulièrement attrayant. On y sert surtout une cuisine japonaise et notamment du poisson cru de grande qualité. Un service de plats à emporter a été mis en place depuis peu et on prévoit également d'ouvrir une boutique de vêtements japonais et d'accessoires de décoration.

L'estetica nipponica incontra il design italiano in un sofisticato ristorante asiatico. La posizione del SOMO nell'animato rione di Trastevere dà vita a un contrasto particolarmente interessante. Il suo punto di forza risiede nella cucina giapponese con la preparazione di pietanze a base di pesce crudo della migliore qualità. Da poco ha aperto anche un take-away. È prevista inoltre l'apertura di un negozio con vestiti e accessori per la casa giapponesi.

Sora Lella

Via Ponte 4 Capi, 16
00186 Rome
Isola Tiberina
Phone: +39 / 06 / 6 86 16 01
www.soralella.com

Opening hours: Open Wed–Sat for lunch and dinner, Tue just dinner, Mon closed
Prices: €€
Cuisine: Italian
Public transportation: Bus to Petroselli or Piazza Monte Savello
Map: No. 15

The Isola Tiberina is only 886 feet long and is connected to Trastevere on the one and Rome's Jewish quarter on the other side via two bridges. Connoisseurs of the Cucina Romana will not want to miss the restaurant Sora Lella, located in an impressive medieval tower. The menu "Tipica Romana" is a cross section of what the Roman cuisine has to offer and is so successful that the owners of the restaurant have recently opened a branch in New York.

Gerade einmal 270 Meter lang ist die Isola Tiberina, die durch zwei Brücken mit Trastevere auf der einen Seite und dem jüdischen Viertel Roms auf der anderen Seite verbunden ist. Anziehungspunkt für alle Liebhaber der Cucina Romana ist das Restaurant Sora Lella in einem eindrucksvollen mittelalterlichen Turm. Das Degustationsmenü „Tipica Romana" zeigt einen Querschnitt der römischen Küche, die so erfolgreich ist, dass die Besitzer gerade in New York eine Dependance eröffneten.

L'Isola Tiberina, reliée par deux ponts au Trastevere, d'une part, et au quartier juif, d'autre part, fait à peine 270 mètres de long. Le restaurant Sora Lella, logé dans une impressionnante tour médiévale, est le point d'attraction de tous les amateurs de la Cucina Romana. Le menu dégustation « Tipica Romana » donne un aperçu de la cuisine romaine. Cette formule a connu un tel succès que les propriétaires viennent d'ouvrir une succursale à New York.

L'Isola Tiberina, unita da due ponti a Trastevere da un lato e al ghetto ebraico dall'altro, è lunga appena 270 metri. Attrazione per tutti gli amanti della cucina romana è il ristorante Sora Lella all'interno di un'imponente torre medioevale. Il menù di degustazione "tipica romana" mostra uno spaccato della cucina romana che ha riscosso un tale successo, che il proprietario ha aperto una filiale a New York.

CLUBS, LOUNGES & BARS

AlexanderPlatz JazzClub

Via Ostia, 9
00192 Rome
Centro Storico
Phone: +39 / 06 / 58 33 57 81
www.alexanderplatz.it

Opening hours: Daily from 8 pm, live concerts start at 10 pm
Prices: €€
Public transportation: Metro Ottaviano / Cipro
Map: No. 16

Russell James' Special Tip

Descend underground to Rome's oldest jazz club, which serves cold drinks and hot tunes in shabby-chic confines decorated with past performers' autographs.

Famous jazz musicians such as Wynton Marsalis and Lionel Hampton have played here. Trumpet legend Chet Baker even gave one of his last concerts in the vaults of this venue. AlexanderPlatz, located near the Vatican, is the oldest and best jazz club in Italy, as autographs painted on the walls by the world's most famous jazz musicians vividly testify. The vintage interior underlines the inspiring atmosphere.

Jazzgrößen wie Wynton Marsalis und Lionel Hampton spielten hier. Trompeterlegende Chet Baker gab in den Gewölben sogar eines seiner letzten Konzerte. AlexanderPlatz nahe dem Vatikan ist der älteste und beste Jazzklub Italiens. Autogramme, von den berühmtesten Jazzmusikern der Welt an die Wände gepinselt, legen davon beredtes Zeugnis ab. Das Vintage-Interieur unterstreicht die inspirierende Atmosphäre.

De grands noms du jazz comme Wynton Marsalis et Lionel Hampton sont passés par ici. Le trompettiste légendaire Chet Baker a même donné l'un de ses derniers concerts dans la cave voûtée. L'AlexanderPlatz, près du Vatican, est l'un des plus anciens clubs de jazz d'Italie et, de surcroît, l'un des meilleurs. De nombreux autographes griffonnés sur les murs par les musiciens de jazz les plus célèbres du monde en sont une preuve éloquente. La décoration intérieure vintage accentue l'atmosphère dépaysante.

I grandi del jazz, come Wynton Marsalis e Lionel Hampton, hanno suonato qui. Il leggendario trombettista Chet Baker ha addirittura tenuto sotto queste volte uno dei suoi ultimi concerti. L'AlexanderPlatz, nei pressi del Vaticano, è il più antico e il migliore jazz club d'Italia, come testimoniano gli autografi dei più celebri musicisti jazz del mondo appesi alle pareti. Gli interni vintage sottolineano l'atmosfera creativa.

I have blisters on me fingers!
Jeff Berlin

HAPPY "19"!
Danny Gottlieb
8-11-01

Freni e Frizioni

Via del Politeama, 4-6
00153 Rome
Trastevere
Phone: +39 / 06 / 45 49 74 99
www.freniefrizioni.com

Opening hours: Mon–Sun 11 am to 2 am
Prices: €€
Public transportation: Bus to LGT Farnesina / Trilussa
Map: No. 17

Eva Padberg's Special Tip
Come early to this boho hip nightspot for a potent cocktail and complimentary buffet; stay late, and the party spills onto the courtyard.

Rome's hippest place to be at the start of the evening. Young artists frequent the Freni e Frizioni near the Ponte Sisto in Trastevere. It owes its unusual name (brakes and clutches) to the fact that it used to be a garage. Its specialty is the Aperitivo. From seven o'clock onwards one can complement the (paid for) cocktails with a helping from to the (free) buffet. The place is accordingly packed.

Roms angesagtester Ort für den frühen Abend. Junge Künstler und Kreative frequentieren das Freni e Frizioni an der Ponte Sisto in Trastevere, das seinen ungewöhnlichen Namen (Bremsen und Kupplungen) der Tatsache verdankt, dass das Gebäude früher eine KFZ-Werkstatt beherbergte. Spezialität ist der Aperitivo. Ab sieben Uhr darf man sich zu den – bezahlten – Cocktails kostenlos vom Buffet bedienen. Entsprechend drangvoll geht es zu.

L'endroit le plus hip de Rome pour commencer sa soirée. Le Freni e Frizioni, situé près du Ponte Sisto au Trastevere, est fréquenté par de jeunes artistes et doit son nom insolite (freins et embrayages) au fait que l'immeuble abritait autrefois un garage automobile. Sa spécialité est l'apéritif. À partir de 19 heures, on peut se servir gratuitement au buffet pour accompagner le cocktail payant. Il ne faut donc pas s'étonner que cet endroit soit toujours plein à craquer.

Il locale più alla moda della prima serata romana. Giovani artisti e creativi frequentano il Freni e Frizioni, nei pressi di Ponte Sisto a Trastevere, che deve il proprio inconsueto nome al fatto che l'edificio ospitava prima un'autofficina. La specialità del locale sono gli aperitivi. A partire dalle sette ci si può servire a un lauto e affollato buffet con cui accompagnare il proprio cocktail.

E FRIZIONI

Il Palazzetto Wine Bar

Vicolo del Bottino, 8
00187 Rome
Centro Storico
Phone: +39 / 06 / 6 99 34 10 00
www.ilpalazzettoroma.com

Opening hours: Tue–Sun 6 pm until late
Prices: €€
Public transportation: Bus to Spagna (MA)
Map: No. 18

The location right next to the Spanish Steps could not be more spectacular. The small palazzo, which served as a townhouse for a Roman patrician family during the 16th century, is now owned by Roberto E. Wirth, owner of the exclusive Hotel Hassler, who indulges in his intensely personal passion for wine. Following a complete renovation at the end of 2008, the wine bar on the 2nd floor exudes inimitable Italian elegance.

Die Lage direkt an der Spanischen Treppe könnte nicht spektakulärer sein. Im kleinen Palazzo, der im 16. Jahrhundert als Zweitwohnsitz einer römischen Patrizierfamilie diente, frönt Roberto E. Wirth, Besitzer des vornehmen Hotel Hassler, seiner ganz persönlichen Leidenschaft für Wein. Nach einer kompletten Renovierung Ende 2008 zeigt sich die Wine Bar im 2. Stock in unnachahmlicher italienischer Eleganz.

Son emplacement directement à côté de l'Escalier Espagnol ne pourrait être plus spectaculaire. Dans un petit « palazzo », résidence secondaire d'une famille patricienne au XVIe siècle, Roberto E. Wirth, le propriétaire de l'hôtel distingué Hassler, donne libre cours à sa passion, le vin. Entièrement rénové fin 2008, le bar à vins au deuxième étage déploie une élégance italienne inimitable.

La sua posizione, proprio di fronte alla scalinata di Piazza di Spagna, non poteva essere più spettacolare. Nel piccolo palazzo, che nel XVI secolo fungeva da seconda dimora per una famiglia patrizia romana, Roberto E. Wirth, proprietario del signorile Hotel Hassler, si dedica alla propria passione per il vino. Dopo una ristrutturazione generale a fine 2008, il wine bar al secondo piano si presenta con un'eleganza tutta italiana.

Maud

Via Capo d'Africa, 6 Colosseo
00184 Rome
Centro Storico
Phone: +39 / 06 / 77 59 08 09
www.maud-roma.it

Opening hours: Tue–Sun 7pm to 2 am
Prices: €€€
Public transportation: Metro Colosseo
Map: No. 19

Maud is a restaurant, American bar and art gallery in one and is located only a few steps from the Colosseum. The interior is kept in glamorous white. The cuisine, Italian with oriental influences, plays on the theme of salts with different varieties from all over the world on offer. Among them salts from the Himalayas, Australia, Hawaii, or the famous Fleur de Sel from the French Atlantic coast.

Maud ist Restaurant, American Bar und Kunstgalerie in einem und liegt nur wenige Schritte vom Kolosseum entfernt. Das gesamte Interieur ist in glanzvollem Weiß gehalten. Die Küche, italienisch mit orientalischem Einfluss, variiert das Thema Salz. Hier werden Salze aus den unterschiedlichsten Regionen der Welt verkostet, wie zum Beispiel vom Himalaja, aus Australien, Hawaii oder das berühmte Fleur de Sel von der französischen Atlantikküste.

Le Maud, à la fois restaurant, bar américain et galerie d'art, se trouve à quelques pas du Colisée. Le décor intérieur chic joue dans le registre blanc. La cuisine italienne, avec des influences orientales, décline le thème du sel : on y déguste des variétés de sels provenant du monde entier, comme par exemple de l'Himalaya, d'Australie, de Hawaï, ou encore la célèbre fleur de sel de la côte atlantique française.

Maud è ristorante, american bar e galleria d'arte in uno, il tutto a pochi passi dal Colosseo. Gli interni in stile sono completamente bianchi. La cucina, italiana con influssi orientali, propone variazioni sul tema del sale. Qui è possibile degustare sali da tutti gli angoli del mondo, come ad esempio il sale dell'Himalaya, quello australiano, delle Hawaii o il famoso fleur de sel della costa atlantica francese.

CLUBS, LOUNGES & BARS . Maud   105

Salotto 42

Piazza di Pietra, 42
00186 Rome
Centro Storico
Phone: +39 / 06 / 6 78 58 04
www.salotto42.it

Opening hours: Tue–Sat 10 am to 2 am, Sun 10 am to midnight
Prices: €€
Public transportation: Bus to Corso / Minghetti
Map: No. 20

The lounge belonging to Italian and Swedish owners with its vintage furniture from the '50s exudes a relaxed living room atmosphere. Browse art books or fashion magazines under the Murano glass chandelier and join the numerous model friends of the proprietress. Glass panels provide a view of the mighty Corinthian columns of the Temple of Hadrian.

Vintage-Möbel aus den 50er-Jahren sorgen für eine entspannte Wohnzimmeratmosphäre in der Lounge des italienisch-schwedischen Besitzerpaars. Unter dem Lüster aus Murano-Glas kann man in Kunstbänden und Modemagazinen schmökern, wie die Modelkolleginnen der Besitzerin, die das Salotto 42 gerne frequentieren. Durch Glasscheiben schaut man auf die mächtigen korinthischen Säulen des Hadriantempels.

Des meubles vintage des années cinquante créent une ambiance agréable et familière dans le lounge des propriétaires, un couple italo-suédois. Sous le lustre en cristal de Murano, on peut feuilleter à sa guise des livres d'art et des magazines de mode, comme le font les mannequins, collègues de la propriétaire, qui fréquentent volontiers le Salotto 42. À travers les vitres on a une belle vue sur les imposantes colonnes corinthiennes du temple d'Hadrien.

Nella lounge della coppia di proprietari italo-svedese, il mobilio vintage degli anni Cinquanta ricrea l'atmosfera rilassata di un salotto. Sotto il lampadario in vetro di Murano è possibile perdersi in libri d'arte e riviste di moda, come fanno le modelle – colleghe della proprietaria – che frequentano il Salotto 42. Dalle vetrate si vedono le imponenti colonne corinzie del tempio di Adriano.

Société Lutèce Roma

Piazza di Montevecchio, 17
00186 Rome
Centro Storico
Phone: +39 / 06 / 68 30 14 72
www.societe-lutece.it

Opening hours: Daily 6 pm to 2 am
Prices: €
Public transportation: Bus to Zanardelli
Map: No. 21

Young stylish Romans who want to get away from the touristy nightlife of the Campo de' Fiori flee to the little-known hip neighborhood behind Santa Maria della Pace. The Société Lutèce, owned by Freni e Frizioni, is a favorite spot. Again, there is an early evening buffet with pasta salads, risottos, and vegetables on offer to go with the aperitivo.

Junge, stylische Römer, denen das Nachtleben rund um den Campo de' Fiori zu touristisch geworden ist, flüchten sich in das versteckte Szeneviertel hinter Santa Maria della Pace. Liebster Ankerplatz dort ist die Société Lutece, Schwesterlokal des Freni e Frizioni. Auch dort wird am frühen Abend zum Aperitivo ein Buffet mit Pastasalaten, Risottos und Gemüse zum Dippen angeboten.

Quand les jeunes romains branchés trouvent que la vie nocturne aux alentours du Campo de' Fiori devient trop touristique, ils se réfugient dans le quartier caché derrière Santa Maria della Pace, seulement connu des initiés. La Société Lutèce, sœur du Freni e Frizioni, en est le local le plus populaire. Ici aussi, en début de soirée, on peut accompagner son apéritif d'un buffet composé de salades de pâtes, de risottos et de légumes.

I giovani trendy di Roma, per i quali la vita notturna intorno a Campo de' Fiori è diventata troppo turistica, si rifugiano nel quartiere alla moda dietro Santa Maria della Pace. Il ritrovo preferito lì è la Société Lutèce, locale gemello del Freni e Frizioni. Anche qui a inizio serata viene offerto con l'aperitivo un buffet con insalata di pasta, risotti e verdure in pinzimonio.

SHOPS

Azi

Via Luciano Manara, 7
00153 Rome
Trastevere
Phone: +39 / 06 / 5 81 86 99

Opening hours: Mon–Sat 10 am to 2 pm and 4 pm to 8 pm
Products: Kitchen Accessories and home decoration
Public transportation: Bus to Trastevere / Mastai
Map: No. 22

Azi in Trastevere has as little to do with your ordinary culinary shop as an espresso with drip coffee. Not only the home accessories but also the thoroughly practical kitchen utensils, display only the finest Italian design. Owner Mario Azi is constantly searching for new and exclusive items to jazz up your home.

Mit einem herkömmlichen Küchenladen hat Azi in Trastevere ungefähr genauso viel zu tun wie Espresso mit Filterkaffee. Das Nonplusultra an angesagtem italienischen Design spiegelt sich in jedem der präsentierten Wohnaccessoires wie auch in den durchaus praktischen Küchenutensilien wider. Besitzer Mario Azi ist ständig auf der Suche nach neuen exklusiven Stücken, mit denen man die häuslichen vier Wände aufpeppen kann.

L'Azi, situé au Trastevere, ressemble autant à un magasin traditionnel d'accessoires et ustensiles de cuisine qu'un espresso à un café-filtre. Le nec plus ultra du design italien le plus tendance se retrouve dans chaque article de décoration et dans le moindre ustensile de cuisine, qui n'en oublie pas toutefois d'être pratique à l'usage. Mario Azi, le propriétaire, est constamment en quête de nouveautés exclusives, susceptibles d'agrémenter votre intérieur.

Azi, a Trastevere, non ha nulla a che vedere con un comune negozio di articoli da cucina. Il nonplusultra del design italiano più attuale si riflette in ognuno degli accessori per la casa in vendita, nonché negli utensili da cucina incredibilmente pratici. Il proprietario, Mario Azi, è sempre in cerca di nuovi pezzi esclusivi con i quali è possibile aggiungere un tocco speciale alla propria casa.

La Bottega del Cioccolato

Via Leonina, 82
00184 Rome
Centro Storico
Phone: +39 / 06 / 4 82 14 73
www.labottegadelcioccolato.it

Opening hours: Closed in summer
Products: Over 50 types of chocolate
Public transportation: Bus to Cavour / Annibaldi
Map: No. 23

Eva Padberg's Special Tip
Luscious chocolates and candied violets make this sweets store a must. But remember, the unrefrigerated shop is closed come summer.

Contrary to the new stylish chocolate shops which crop up all over the place, the Bottega can look back on a long tradition. The secrets of making the perfect chocolate and the passion for this sweet craft has been handed down the family Proietti for generations. Its specialty is a mini Colosseum made from chocolate.

Im Unterschied zu den durchdesignten Schokoladengeschäften, die allerorts wie Pilze aus dem Boden schießen, kann die Bottega auf eine lange Tradition zurückblicken. Seit Generationen werden die Geheimnisse der perfekten Schokoladeherstellung und die Passion für dieses süße Handwerk in der Besitzerfamilie Proietti weitergegeben. Spezialität ist ein Minikolosseum aus Schokolade.

À la différence des boutiques de chocolat design qui prolifèrent un peu partout, la Bottega s'appuie sur une longue tradition. Chez la famille Proietti, en effet, les secrets de la fabrication parfaite du chocolat et la passion pour cet artisanat sont transmis de génération en génération. La spécialité est un Colisée miniature en chocolat.

A differenza delle tante cioccolaterie dal design studiato nei minimi particolari che nascono come funghi, la Bottega del Cioccolato può vantare una lunga tradizione. Da generazioni i proprietari, la famiglia Proietti, si tramandano i segreti per la perfetta lavorazione del cioccolato e la passione per questa dolcissima arte. La specialità del negozio è un minuscolo Colosseo di cioccolato.

La Perla

Via dei Condotti, 78
00187 Rome
Centro Storico
Phone: +39 / 06 / 69 94 19 34
www.laperla.com

Opening hours: Mon 3 pm to 7 pm, Tue–Sat 10 am to 7 pm
Products: Fashion, lingerie and swimwear
Public transportation: Metro Piazza di Spagna
Map: No. 24

The perfect handiwork applied to top quality lace of its enticing lingerie helped the Italian brand to fame. These days La Perla is a lifestyle brand with collections for both sexes which can be admired in the fine ambiance of its flagship store on the Via Condotti next to other fashion icons such as Armani, Gucci and Prada.

Die handwerklich perfektionierte Verarbeitung von feinster Spitze für verführerische Dessous machte das italienische Wäschelabel berühmt. Längst ist aus La Perla eine Lifestylemarke geworden, mit Bekleidungskollektionen für beide Geschlechter, die im edlen Ambiente des Flagshipstores an der Via Condotti in bester Nachbarschaft zu Armani, Gucci und Prada präsentiert werden.

La confection artisanale de la dentelle la plus fine destinée à des dessous séduisants a rendu célèbre cette marque italienne de lingerie. La Perla est devenue depuis longtemps une marque « life style ». Ses collections, pour les femmes comme pour les hommes, sont présentées dans l'ambiance élégante du magasin vitrine de la marque, sur la Via Condotti, en la bonne compagnie des boutiques Armani, Gucci et Prada.

La lavorazione, perfezionata artigianalmente, dei pizzi più raffinati per creare capi seducenti ha reso famoso questo marchio di abbigliamento intimo. Da molto tempo La Perla è diventato un marchio lifestyle con collezioni di vestiti per uomo e donna, presentati nell'esclusivo ambiente del negozio monomarca in via Condotti, dove è affiancato dalle boutique di Armani, Gucci e Prada.

Libreria del Cinema

Via dei Fienaroli, 31 d
00153 Rome
Trastevere
Phone: +39 / 06 / 5 81 77 24
www.libreriadelcinema.roma.it

Opening hours: Sun–Fri 10 am to 9 pm, Sat 11 am to 11 pm
Products: Books, DVD's, video tapes, music
Public transportation: Bus to Sonnino / San Gallicano
Map: No. 25

Russell James' Special Tip
Film fans flock to this movie heaven to scoop up DVDs and cinema-centric books, then sip strong espressos in the café bar.

A group of friends have perhaps chosen the coolest street in Trastevere to set up their film bookstore which quickly became the meeting place for movie buffs and makers. So do not be surprised when a famous director or script writer is on the prowl. The small café also offers workshops and discussions.

Es ist die vielleicht coolste Straße in Trastevere, die sich eine Gruppe von Freunden für ihren Film-buchladen ausgewählt haben, der in kürzester Zeit zu einem Treffpunkt für Cineasten und Filmemacher geworden ist. Also nicht wundern, wenn man einen bekannten Regisseur oder Drehbuchschreiber beim Stöbern beobachten kann. Auch Workshops und Diskussionsveranstaltungen im kleinen Café werden hier angeboten.

C'est peut être la rue la plus hip du Trastevere qu'un groupe d'amis a choisie pour ouvrir sa librairie du cinéma. Celle-ci est devenue en peu de temps le lieu de rendez-vous des cinéastes et des réalisateurs. Il n'est donc pas rare de tomber sur un metteur en scène connu ou un scénariste feuilletant des volu-mes. Dans le petit café, on propose aussi des workshops et des discussions à thème.

È forse la strada più trendy di tutto Trastevere quella che un gruppo di amici ha scelto per aprire una libreria dedicata al cinema, divenuta in breve tempo un ritrovo per cineasti. Non c'è quindi da mera-vigliarsi se ci si imbatte in un famoso regista o sceneggiatore intento a sfogliare qualche libro. Nella piccola caffetteria si tengono anche workshop e dibattiti.

Nuyorica

Piazza Pollarola, 36-37
00186 Rome
Centro Storico
Phone: +39 / 06 / 68 89 12 43
www.nuyorica.it

Opening hours: Mon–Sat 10 am to 8 pm, Sun 3 pm to 8 pm
Products: Fashion
Public transportation: Bus to Corso Vittorio or Emanuele II
Map: No. 26

Accessories, high heels, and extravagant purses are presented like works of art in this stylish shop. Sofas and well chosen background music make for a relaxed club atmosphere. Perfect prerequisites to create one's own outfit and to try out one or the other hip designer item.

Accessoires, High Heels und ausgefallene Taschen werden in dem durchgestylten Laden wie Kunstwerke präsentiert. Sofas und ausgewählte Hintergrundsmusik sorgen für eine entspannte Klubatmosphäre. Beste Voraussetzungen, um das eigene Outfit rundzuerneuern und wenigstens das eine oder andere Kleidungsstück angesagter Designer anzuprobieren.

Accessoires, talons aiguilles et sacs à main originaux sont mis en scène comme des œuvres d'art dans cette boutique design. Les canapés et une musique de fond bien choisie contribuent à créer une atmosphère détendue de club. Les meilleures conditions, donc, pour renouveler sa garde-robe ou, au moins, essayer l'une ou l'autre création des stylistes à la mode.

In questo negozio alla moda accessori, tacchi alti e borsette a tracolla vengono presentati come fossero opere d'arte. Divani e musica di sottofondo selezionata ricreano l'atmosfera rilassata di un locale notturno: la premessa ideale per rifarsi il look e per provare qualche capo del designer del momento.

La Rinascente

Via del Corso, 189
00187 Rome
Centro Storico
Phone: +39 / 06 / 6 79 76 91
www.rinascente.it

Opening hours: Mon–Sat 9.30 am to 9.30 pm, Sun 10.00 am to 9 pm
Products: Cosmetics, perfume, fashion
Public transportation: Bus to Piazza San Silvestro
Map: No. 27

Rome's oldest department store in a historical Palazzo on the Via del Corso is steeped in tradition and its beautifully preserved Art-Nouveau architecture is worth a visit on its own. Apart from that, the Rinascente has everything to help you make a "bella figura." And that, as we know, takes top priority with all real Romans. Apart from apparel and shoes you will also find wonderful home accessories.

Das älteste Kaufhaus Roms, in einem historischen Palazzo an der Via del Corso, blickt auf eine große Tradition zurück und lohnt schon wegen der wunderbar erhaltenen Jugendstil-Räume einen Besuch. Zudem wird im Rinascente einfach alles geboten, was dabei hilft „Bella Figura" zu machen. Und das hat, wie wir wissen, oberste Priorität bei allen echten Römern. Neben Kleidung und Schuhen gibt es auch Wohnaccessoires.

Logé dans un palazzo historique à la Via del Corso, le plus ancien grand magasin de Rome a une longue tradition et vaut bien une visite, ne serait ce que pour sa magnifique architecture art nouveau merveilleusement conservée. Mais la Rinascente a aussi tout ce qu'il faut pour faire « Bella Figura ». Ce qui est prioritaire, on le sait, pour tout Romain authentique. Outre vêtements et chaussures, on y trouve aussi des articles de décoration.

La Rinascente è il più antico centro commerciale di Roma. Ubicata in un palazzo storico di Via del Corso si rifà a una lunga tradizione e merita di essere vista se non altro per le sale in stile Liberty meravigliosamente conservate. Inoltre qui è possibile trovare tutto il necessario per fare bella figura, cosa che, come sappiamo, è la priorità assoluta di ogni vero romano. Oltre al vestiario e alle scarpe, La Rinascente offre anche articoli per la casa.

Sant' Eustachio

Piazza Sant'Eustachio, 82
00186 Rome
Centro Storico
Phone: +39 / 06 / 68 80 20 48
www.santeustachioilcaffe.it

Opening hours: Daily 8.30 am to 1 am, Sat 8.30 am to 2 am
Products: Coffee (self-roasted), chocolate
Public transportation: Bus to Rinascimento / Largo Argentina
Map: No. 28

Eva Padberg's Special Tip
Caffeinate like a local at this legendary café, where the secret-recipe espresso—made with beans roasted over wood—is impossibly frothy and rich.

The Sant' Eustachio is Rome's oldest coffee roastery and many believe it is also the best. Sacks of coffee and historical photos of coffee plantations document where the house receives its beans from. The big secret and specialty of the house is the "gran caffè" which is made behind a chrome screen to keep out preying eyes. The delicious nougat-filled "dolci" are a must as an accompaniment.

Das Sant' Eustachio ist die älteste Kaffeerösterei Roms und für viele Römer auch die Beste. Kaffee-säcke und historische Fotografien von Kaffeeplantagen zeigen, woher man die Kaffeebohnen bezieht. Ein großes Geheimnis wird indes um die Spezialität des Hauses, den „Gran Caffè" gemacht, der versteckt hinter einem Sichtschutz aus Chrom zubereitet wird. Dazu unbedingt von den köstlichen nugatgefüllten "Dolci" kosten.

Le Sant' Eustachio est le plus ancien torréfacteur de Rome et aussi le meilleur selon beaucoup de Romains. Si des sacs de café et des photos historiques de plantations illustrent la provenance des grains de café, la spécialité de la maison, le « Gran Caffè », est un secret jalousement gardé. On le prépare à l'abri des regards derrière un écran en chrome. Il faut absolument l'accompagner de l'un des délicieux « dolci » fourrés praliné.

Sant' Eustachio è la più antica torrefazione di caffè di Roma e per molti romani è anche la migliore. Sacchi di caffè e fotografie storiche di piantagioni rivelano da dove arrivano i preziosi chicchi. Invece sulla specialità della casa, il "Gran caffè", si mantiene il più stretto riserbo; questo viene preparato lontano da occhi indiscreti dietro uno schermo in cromo. Da non perdere i deliziosi dolci ripieni di nougat.

Sant Eustachio
il caffè
20 SETTEMBRE
SANT EUSTACHIO
URBS MIRABILIS ROMA

TAD

Via del Babuino, 155 a
00187 Rome
Centro Storico
Phone: +39 / 06 / 32 69 51 31
www.taditaly.com

Opening hours: Mon noon to 7.30 pm, Tue–Fri 10.30 am to 8 pm, Sun noon to 8 pm
Products: Furniture, fashion, CD's, hairdresser and café inside the house
Public transportation: Metro Spagna and Flaminio
Map: No. 29

Even if the plethora of art in Rome leaves you with little time to go shopping, you simply must make time for TAD. To start off with, the concept store is situated in one of the city's most beautiful shopping streets, the Via del Babuino. Secondly, cosmopolitans will find two floors full of stylish and tasteful apparel, home accessories and magazines which you will be hard pushed to find elsewhere.

Sollte bei der Fülle an Kunstschätzen, die Rom zu bieten hat, nur noch wenig Zeit für eine Einkaufstour bleiben, dann muss man zu TAD. Erstens liegt der Concept-Store an der Via del Babuino, der vielleicht schönsten Einkaufsstraße Roms. Und zweitens finden Kosmopoliten auf zwei Stockwerken eine Fülle an stilvollen und geschmackvollen Kleidungsstücken, Wohnaccessoires und Magazinen, die man anderswo erst mühsam aufstöbern muss.

Même si, en raison de la quantité d'œuvres d'art qu'offre Rome, il ne vous reste que peu de temps pour le shopping, vous ne devez pas manquer le TAD. D'une part parce que ce magasin concept est situé Via del Babuino, l'une des plus belles rues commerçantes de Rome. Et d'autre part parce que, sur deux étages, il propose aux cosmopolites des vêtements stylés de bon goût, des articles de décoration, et aussi des magazines presque introuvables ailleurs.

Se tra una visita ai tesori artistici di Roma e l'altra dovesse rimanere un po' di tempo per fare shopping, TAD è il posto giusto: non solo perché questo concept store si trova in via del Babuino, forse la via più bella in tutta Roma per fare shopping, ma anche perché i cosmopoliti possono trovare nei due piani del negozio una ricca scelta di capi d'abbigliamento, accessori per la casa e riviste di tendenza all'insegna dello stile e del buon gusto, difficili da trovare altrove.

Vestiti Usati Cinzia

Via del Governo Vecchio, 45
00186 Rome
Centro Storico
Phone: +39 / 06 / 6 83 29 45

Opening hours: Mon–Sat 10 am to 8 pm, Sun 2 pm to 8 pm
Products: Second hand fashion and accessories
Public transportation: Bus to Corso Vittorio Emanuele / Navona
Map: No. 30

All fans of the retro chic of the '60s and '70s will find Cinzia's second-hand store on the Via del Governo Vecchio a true treasure trove. The owner stumbles over original sunglasses, shoes, vintage jeans, and purses almost exclusively on her visits to flea markets and jumble sales. Her favorite items such as the Mary Quant sunglasses are displayed in a small glass cabinet and are not for sale.

Für alle, die nach dem Retrochic der 60er- und 70er-Jahre suchen, ist Cinzias Secondhandladen in der Via del Governo Vecchio eine wahre Fundgrube. Die Besitzerin entdeckt die originellen Sonnenbrillen, Schuhe, Vintage-Jeans und Taschen fast ausschließlich beim Stöbern auf Flohmärkten. Ihre unverkäuflichen Lieblingsstücke, wie die Mary-Quant-Sonnenbrillen, präsentiert sie in einer kleinen Glasvitrine.

Pour tous les amateurs du rétro chic des années soixante et soixante-dix, cette boutique de vêtements d'occasion, située Via del Governo Vecchio, est une véritable aubaine. C'est presque exclusivement sur les marchés aux puces que la propriétaire déniche les lunettes de soleil, les chaussures, les jeans vintage et les sacs à main. Ses pièces favorites, comme par exemple les lunettes de soleil Mary Quant, ne sont pas à vendre ; elle les présente dans une petite vitrine.

Per tutti coloro che cercano la moda rétro degli anni Sessanta e Settanta, il negozio di vestiti usati di Cinzia in via del Governo Vecchio è una vera è propria miniera. La proprietaria trova occhiali da sole, scarpe, jeans vintage e borse quasi esclusivamente frugando per i mercatini delle pulci. I suoi articoli preferiti, rigorosamente non in vendita, come gli occhiali da sole di Mary Quant, fanno bella mostra di sé in una vetrinetta.

Volpetti

Via Marmorata, 47
00153 Rome
Testaccio
Phone: +39 / 06 / 5 74 23 52
www.volpetti.com

Opening hours: Mon–Sat 8 am to 2 pm and 5 pm to 8.15 pm
Products: Cheese, wine, ham, salami
Public transportation: Metro B Piramide
Map: No. 31

Eva Padberg's Special Tip
Visit this cramped deli crammed with dangling meats and cheeses in the morning before the crowds descend, ensuring counterworkers' full attention.

If Cockaigne were on the River Tiber, it would look like Volpetti. The delicatessen in the hip Testaccio neighborhood offers a plethora of Italian hams, salamis, rare cheeses, wines, home made pasta, and other delicacies which have every fan of the Italian cuisine jump for joy. So much the better that one can taste the little tidbits in the deli next door.

Läge das Schlaraffenland am Tiber, müsste es so ausschauen wie das Volpetti. Der Delikatessenladen im angesagten Viertel Testaccio bietet eine Fülle an italienischen Schinken, Salamis, seltenen Käsesorten, Weinen, hausgemachter Pasta und anderen Delikatessen, die jedem Liebhaber italienischer Küche das Herz höher schlagen lassen. Umso besser, dass man die Köstlichkeiten gleich nebenan im Deli probieren kann.

Si le pays de cocagne se trouvait au bord du Tibre, il ressemblerait sans doute au Volpetti. Cette épicerie fine, située dans le quartier tendance du Testaccio, propose un riche assortiment de jambons italiens, salamis, fromages rares, vins, pâtes maison et autres délices qui font battre le cœur des amateurs de cuisine italienne et que l'on peut déguster au Deli, juste à côté.

Se il paese della cuccagna si trovasse lungo il Tevere, avrebbe l'aspetto di Volpetti. Questa gastronomia nel rione di tendenza del Testaccio offre un'enorme varietà di prosciutti, salami, formaggi particolari, vini, pasta fatta in casa e altre leccornie, tutti di provenienza nazionale e in grado di sedurre ogni amante della cucina italiana. Come se non bastasse, è possibile provare le prelibatezze direttamente di fianco al locale.

HIGHLIGHTS

Campo de' Fiori

Campo de' Fiori
00186 Rome
Centro Storico

Public transportation: Bus to Corso Vittorio Emanuele / Navona
Map: No. 32

Russell James' Special Tip
Hit the lively piazza in the morn to buy fresh produce; come afternoon, vendors give way to impromptu soccer games.

This is Rome's busiest and probably most colorful market. In the morning vegetable and fruit grocers peddle their fresh wares vociferously. In the evening, the noise level does not lower when young Romans gather on the Campo de' Fiori and start crowding into the bars from seven o'clock onwards. The statue of Giordano Bruno, who was executed by inquisitors in 1600, keeps a watch on the proceedings.

Der belebteste und wohl farbenprächtigste Markt Roms. Morgens bieten Gemüse- und Obsthändler lautstark ihre taufrischen Waren an. Abends rührt der nicht minder hohe Geräuschpegel von jungen Römern, die den Campo de' Fiori zu ihrem Treffpunkt erkoren haben und ab 19 Uhr die Bars bevölkern. Über allem wacht die Statue Giordano Brunos, den die Inquisitoren im Jahr 1600 hier hinrichten ließen.

Le marché de Rome le plus animé et le plus coloré. Le matin, les marchands proposent en s'égosillant leurs fruits et légumes encore humides de rosée. Le soir venu, la place retentit sous les conversations tout aussi bruyantes des jeunes Romains, qui ont fait du Campo de' Fiori leur lieu de rendez-vous et remplissent les bars à partir de 19 heures. Sous le regard attentif de la statue de Giordano Bruno, qui fut brûlé ici par les inquisiteurs en l'an 1600.

Il mercato più amato e colorato di Roma. Qui la mattina i commercianti di frutta e verdura offrono con voce stentorea i loro prodotti freschissimi. La sera il rumore non diminuisce: i giovani di Roma hanno eletto Campo de' Fiori a proprio ritrovo e a partire dalle 19.00 gremiscono i bar. Vigila su questo trambusto la statua di Giordano Bruno giustiziato qui dall'inquisizione nel 1600.

Casa del Cinema

Largo Marcello Mastroianni, 1
00197 Rome
Villa Borghese
Phone: +39 / 06 / 42 36 01
www.casadelcinema.it

Opening hours: Oct–March 10 am to 8 pm, June–Sept 10 am to midnight
Public transportation: Metro Spagna, Barberini, Villa Borghese, Flaminio, Piazza del Popolo
Map: No. 33

Those fed up with multiplex cinemas will think they are in heaven. The Casa del Cinema in the Casina delle Rose, one of the Villa Borghese's most charming buildings, has established itself as a center for all things cinema since it opened in 2004. The discerning program is complemented by discussions with filmmakers and includes a DVD and film library.

Multiplex geschädigte Popcornhasser werden hier ihren persönlichen Kinohimmel finden. Die Casa del Cinema in der Casina delle Rose, einem der anmutigsten Anwesen der Villa Borghese, konnte sich seit ihrer Eröffnung 2004 als Zentrum für Filmkunst etablieren. Das anspruchsvolle Programm beinhaltet auch Diskussionen mit Filmschaffenden. Mit DVD- und cineastischer Bibliothek.

Les cinéphiles ennemis du pop-corn et lassés du multiplex trouveront ici leur bonheur. La Casa del Cinema, dans la Casina delle Rose, l'une des propriétés les plus charmantes de la Villa Borghese, s'est établie depuis son ouverture en 2004 comme centre de la cinématographie. Le programme exigeant comprend également des débats avec des réalisateurs. Il est pourvu d'une bibliothèque multimédias.

Coloro che odiano i multiplex con i loro secchielli di popcorn, troveranno qui il paradiso cinematografico. La Casa del Cinema all'interno della Casina delle Rose, una delle tenute più amene di Villa Borghese, si è affermata come centro dell'arte cinematografica fin dalla sua inaugurazione nel 2004. Il suo ricco programma comprende anche incontri con registi. Dispone inoltre di una videoteca e di una cineteca.

Centrale Montemartini

Via Ostiense, 106
00154 Rome
Garbatella
Phone: +39 / 06 / 5 74 80 30
www.centralemontemartini.org

Opening hours: Tue–Sun 9 am to 7 pm
Public transportation: Metro B Garbatella
Map: No. 34

Russell James' Special Tip

Industry meets art at this electric plant transformed into a museum; don't miss the machine room where Greek statues are juxtaposed with ancient contraptions.

400 antique statues are presented in front of mighty turbines. The former electricity station Montemartini was supposed to be a stopover exhibition area for a period when the museums on the Capitol were renovated. The contrast of antique works of art and industrial design proved to be so interesting, however, that the former electric plant was transformed into a permanent exhibition space.

400 antike Statuen präsentiert vor mächtigen Turbinen. Das ehemalige Elektrizitätswerk Montemartini sollte als Provisorium für einen Teil der Sammlung dienen, als die Kapitolinischen Museen renoviert wurden. Der Kontrast von antiker Ästhetik und Industriedesign erwies sich als so spannend, dass sich das frühere Elektrizitätswerk einen ständigen Platz in der römischen Museumslandschaft erobern konnte.

400 statues antiques dressées devant un décor de gigantesques turbines. Au départ, l'ancienne centrale électrique de Montemartini était censée recueillir provisoirement une partie des collections du musée du Capitole lors de sa rénovation. Or, le contraste entre l'esthétique antique et le design industriel s'avéra si intéressant que la centrale Montemartini a trouvé une place permanente dans le paysage des musées romains.

400 statue antiche presentate di fronte a possenti turbine. L'ex centrale elettrica di Montemartini doveva fungere da soluzione provvisoria per una parte della collezione dei Musei Capitolini durante la loro ristrutturazione, ma il contrasto tra l'estetica antica e il design industriale si dimostrò talmente riuscito che l'ex centrale elettrica è riuscita a conquistarsi un posto fisso nel panorama dei musei romani.

Colosseum

Piazza del Colosseo
00184 Rome
Centro Storico

Opening hours: Daily 9 am to sunset (last entry 1 hour before closing)
Public transportation: Metro B Colosseo
Map: No. 35

Roman emperors made sure their people were fed and entertained. The place for the latter was the Colosseum, inaugurated in 80 AD. The imposing building serves as archetype for all sporting venues to this day and seated about 50,000 spectators. Following renovation one can once again tour the underground gladiator dungeons and view the sophisticated stage machinery.

„Brot und Spiele" lautete die Formel, mit der die römischen Kaiser das Volk zu lenken pflegten. Ort der blutigen Spektakel war das 80 nach Christus eingeweihte Kolosseum, dessen idealer Bau bis heute Vorbild aller Sportarenen ist. 50 000 Zuschauern bot das imposante Bauwerk Platz. Nach Restaurierungsarbeiten kann man wieder die unterirdischen Verliese der Gladiatoren und die ausgefeilte Bühnentechnik besichtigen.

« Du pain et des jeux », telle était la formule avec laquelle les empereurs romains dirigeaient le peuple. Le Colisée, inauguré en 80 après Jésus-Christ, était le cadre de spectacles sanglants. Son architecture parfaite est jusqu'à nos jours le modèle de toutes les arènes sportives. L'imposante construction pouvait accueillir 50 000 spectateurs. Après des travaux de rénovation, on peut à nouveau visiter les oubliettes des gladiateurs et une machinerie sophistiquée.

"Panem et circenses". Questa sententia riassume il principio secondo cui gli imperatori romani pilotavano il popolo. Il Colosseo fu inaugurato nell'80 d. C., come sede per sanguinari spettacoli. La sua struttura viene oggi ripresa idealmente a modello per tutti gli stadi e i palazzi dello sport. L'imponente opera poteva ospitare 50.000 spettatori. Dopo i lavori di restauro è nuovamente possibile visitare le segrete sotterranee dei gladiatori e l'elaborata scenotecnica.

Forum Romanum

Via dei Fori Imperiali
00185 Rome
Centro Storico

Opening hours: Nov–Feb 8.30 am to 4.30 pm, March until 5.30 pm, April–Sept until 7 pm, Oct until 6.30 pm
Public transportation: Metro B Colosseo, Bus via Fori Imperiali
Map: No. 36

This was once the place in the Curia where Cicero held his speeches that moved the ancient world, and where Cesar overcame his adversaries. The Roman Forum, once the center of the Roman Empire, nowadays resembles an impressive archaeological park with columns, ruins of temples, statues, and triumphal arches. Here every stone has a story to tell and the ancient world comes alive.

Einmal genau an der Stelle in der Kurie stehen, wo Cicero seine, die antike Welt bewegenden, Reden hielt und Caesar seine Widersacher bezwang. Das Forum Romanum, einst Zentrum des römischen Weltreichs, ist heute ein beeindruckender archäologischer Park mit Säulen, Tempelruinen, Statuen und Triumphbögen. Hier erzählt jeder Stein eine Geschichte und die Antike wird hautnah erlebbar.

Qui ne rêve de visiter une fois la curie, là exactement où Cicéron tenait ses discours qui émouvaient le monde antique et là où César triompha de ses adversaires. Le Forum Romain, jadis le centre de l'Empire Romain, est un magnifique parc archéologique aujourd'hui, jalonné de colonnes et de vestiges de temples, de statues et d'arcs de triomphe. Ici, chaque pierre raconte une histoire et fait revivre l'Antiquité.

Il Foro Romano si trova esattamente dove un tempo sorgeva la Curia. Qui Cicerone teneva le sue orazioni, capaci di commuovere l'intero mondo antico, e Cesare annientava i propri avversari; un tempo esso era il centro dell'Impero romano, oggi è un impressionante parco archeologico con colonne, rovine di templi, statue e archi di trionfo. Qui ogni pietra racconta la sua storia e il mondo dell'antichità ritorna a vivere.

Galleria Nazionale d'Arte Moderna (GNAM)

Viale delle Belle Arti 131
00196 Rome
Flaminio
Phone: +39 / 06 / 32 29 82 21
www.gnam.arti.beniculturali.it

Opening hours: Tue–Sun 8.30 am to 7.30 pm
Public transportation: Tram Galleria d'Arte Moderna
Map: No. 37

The museum, located in a neoclassical palazzo, is somewhat eclipsed by the Museum Borghese on the other side of the park. As a result one can roam the 75 rooms of the GNAM quite freely—a luxury the crowded city seldom affords. It harbors the largest collection of Italian art of the 19th and 20th centuries. An insider tip is the museum's café, which proffers a beautiful view of the park.

Das Museum in einem neoklassizistischen Palazzo steht ein wenig im Schatten des Museums Borghese auf der anderen Seite des Parks. Deswegen kann man die 75 Säle des GNAM ungestört durchstreifen, was im überlaufenen Rom selten ist. Es beherbergt die größte Sammlung italienischer Kunst des 19. und 20. Jahrhunderts. Ein Geheimtipp ist das Museumscafé mit einem wunderbaren Blick in den Park.

Logé dans un palazzo néoclassique, ce musée est un peu éclipsé par la présence du musée Borghese, de l'autre côté du parc. C'est pour cela que l'on peut visiter tranquillement les 75 salles du GNAM, chose plutôt rare dans la Rome surpeuplée. Il abrite la plus grande collection d'art italien des XIXe et XXe siècles. À ne pas manquer non plus le café du musée, avec sa merveilleuse vue sur le parc. C'est un vrai tuyau !

Questo museo, la cui sede è all'interno di un palazzo in stile neoclassicistico, rimane un po' all'ombra del Museo Borghese dall'altra parte del parco. Ciò permette di visitare indisturbati le 75 sale del GNAM, esperienza assai rara nell'affollata Capitale. Esso ospita la più grande collezione di opere d'arte del XIX e del XX secolo. Pochi conoscono il caffè del museo con la sua meravigliosa vista sul parco.

Museo d'Arte Contemporanea di Roma (MACRO)

Via Reggio Emilia 54
00198 Rome
Nomentano
Phone: +39 / 06 / 6 71 07 04 00
www.macro.roma.museum

Opening hours: Tue–Sun 9 am to 7 pm
Public transportation: Tram Viale Regina Margherita / Nizza
Map: No. 38

The ancient legacy was so overwhelming that it took a long time to find an appropriate place for modern art. The MACRO is located in the former Peroni brewery which is complemented by an ingenious new building by French architect Odile Decq. Among others one can marvel at Scuola di Piazza del Popolo and Arte Povera pieces; the latter a style which came into being in the '60s.

Das antike Erbe erwies sich als so übermächtig, dass es lange dauerte, bis man am Tiber einen angemessenen Ort für moderne Kunst gestaltete. Das MACRO ist im Gebäude der ehemaligen Peroni-Brauerei zu finden, dem die französischen Architektin Odile Decq einen kongenialen Neubau zur Seite stellte. Gezeigt werden unter anderem Werke der Scuola di Piazza del Popolo und der Arte Povera, einer Kunstrichtung, die sich in den 60er-Jahren formierte.

L'héritage antique s'imposait de telle manière qu'il a fallu beaucoup de temps avant de pouvoir aménager sur les bords du Tibre un cadre digne de l'art moderne. Une extension de même caractère, conçue par l'architecte française Odile Decq, a été construite à côté du MACRO, installé lui-même dans le bâtiment de l'ancienne brasserie Peroni. On peut y admirer, entre autres, des œuvres de la Scuola di Piazza del Popolo et de l'Arte Povera, un style qui surgit dans les années soixante.

L'eredità antica si dimostrò talmente importante che passò molto tempo prima che lungo il Tevere potesse sorgere un luogo adeguato per l'arte contemporanea. Il MACRO ha la propria sede all'interno dell'ex stabilimento della Peroni a cui l'architetto francese Odile Decq ha fornito una sistemazione congeniale. In particolare, qui è possibile vedere le opere della scuola Scuola di Piazza del Popolo e dell'Arte Povera, una delle tendenze formatesi nel corso degli anni Sessanta.

Pantheon

Piazza della Rotonda 116
00186 Rome
Centro Storico

Opening hours: Mon–Sat 8.30 am to 7.30 pm, Sun 9 am to 6 pm, public holidays 9 am to 1 pm
Public transportation: Bus to Senato
Map: No. 39

Nobody who enters this miracle of ancient architecture can fail to be overawed by the august setting. The Pantheon's dome was the world's largest for a good 1,500 years. Only a ray of light passing through the 26-feet-wide oculus lights the huge interior. It is not so often that man is so humbled by his surroundings as he is here.

Niemand, der dieses Wunderwerk antiker Architektur betritt, kann sich der erhabenen Aura dieses Ortes entziehen. Gut eineinhalb Jahrtausende war die Kuppel des Pantheons die weltweit größte. Nur ein Lichtstrahl, der durch den 8 Meter messenden Okulus fällt, erhellt den gewaltigen Innenraum. Wohl selten hat der Mensch das Gefühl, so winzig klein zu sein wie hier.

Il est impossible, pour qui pénètre dans cette merveille de l'architecture antique, de se soustraire à l'aura majestueuse de cet endroit. Pendant près de 1 500 ans, la coupole du Panthéon fut la plus grande du monde. Un unique rai de lumière, qui pénètre par un oculus de 8 mètres de diamètre, éclaire l'intérieur monumental. Il n'est guère d'endroits où l'homme se sent aussi petit.

Chiunque entri in questa meraviglia architettonica dell'antichità non potrà sottrarsi alla sua aura sublime. Oltre un secolo e mezzo fa la cupola del Pantheon era la più grande al mondo. Solamente un fascio di luce, proveniente dall'oculo di 8 metri, schiarisce gli immensi spazi interni. Capita raramente di sentirsi così piccoli!

Piazza di Spagna

Piazza di Spagna
00187 Rome
Centro Storico

Public transportation: Bus to Spagna (MA)
Map: No. 40

The Piazza di Spagna with the famous Spanish Steps resembles an opulent movie setting—ideal for photo shootings and tried and tested by numerous tourists. The Piazza's glamour enraptured English romantic poets John Keats and Lord Byron, who both lived in a manor directly next to the Spanish Steps.

Einer opulenten Filmkulisse gleicht die Piazza di Spagna mit der berühmten Spanischen Treppe – bestens geeignet für Fotoshootings, was auch zahlreiche japanische Reisegruppen zu schätzen wissen. Dem Glamour dieses Platzes tut das keinen Abbruch. Den liebten schon die englischen Romantiker wie John Keats oder der exzentrische Lord Byron, die ein Stadtpalais direkt an der Spanischen Treppe bewohnten.

La Piazza di Spagna, avec le célèbre escalier monumental, ressemble au décor fastueux d'un film. Cadre idéal pour des séances photo, cette place est très appréciée aussi des nombreux groupes de touristes japonais, ce qui ne ternit pas son glamour. Les romantiques anglais comme John Keats ou l'excentrique Lord Byron déjà, qui résidaient dans palais attenant à l'escalier de la Trinità dei Monti, étaient tombés sous son charme.

Piazza di Spagna, con la sua celeberrima scalinata, è simile a una sfarzosa scenografia. Il lugo ideale per servizi fotografici, come ben sanno le schiere di turisti giapponesi, che non riescono peraltro a pregiudicarne il fattore glamour. Questa piazza era amata già dai romantici inglesi quali John Keats o l'eccentrico Lord Byron, che abitavano un palazzo affacciato sulla scalinata di Trinità dei Monti.

Pincio

Piazzale Napoleone
00187 Rome
Centro Storico

Public transportation: Metro and bus to Flaminio
Map: No. 41

Between 1809 and 1814 Giuseppe Valadier created the terraced gardens above the Piazza del Popolo that offer a dreamlike view over the roofs of Rome, which is crowned by the all dominating dome of St. Peter's Basilica. It's simply breathtaking during the evening, when the setting sun pours its golden light over red roofs and ocher-colored façades.

Giuseppe Valadier schuf 1809–1814 die terrassenförmigen Gärten oberhalb der Piazza del Popolo, von denen sich ein traumhafter Blick über Roms Dachlandschaft bis zur alles dominierenden Kuppel des Petersdoms eröffnet. Zum Niederknien schön am Abend, wenn die untergehende Sonne Ziegeldächer und ockerfarbene Hausfassaden mit goldenem Licht übergießt.

Giuseppe Valadier créa entre 1809 et 1814 les jardins en terrasses qui surplombent la Piazza del Popolo, et d'où l'on a une vue de rêve sur les toits de Rome, jusqu'à la coupole de la cathédrale Saint-Pierre qui domine la ville. Le spectacle est inoubliable le soir, lorsque le soleil couchant baigne d'une lumière dorée les toits de tuiles et les façades ocre des maisons.

Tra il 1809 e il 1814 Giuseppe Valadier realizzò il giardino terrazzato sopra Piazza del Popolo da cui si apre una vista spettacolare sui tetti di Roma fino all'imponente cupola di San Pietro. Perfetto di sera, quando il sole tramonta sui tetti di tegole e sulle facciate ocra delle case inondandoli di luce dorata.

Trastevere

Trastevere

Public transportation: Tram Belli
Map: No. 42

Eva Padberg's Special Tip
To see how locals live, hit this winding, lively neighborhood featuring an open-air market and grand churches like the Basilica di Santa Maria Maggiore.

Narrow alleyways full of nooks and crannies and ocher colored houses create an ambiance which seems to attract all things creative. Always known for its bohemian character, the district on the other side of the River Tiber—the literal translation of Trastevere—has turned into Rome's hippest neighborhood full of fashionable small shops, cafés, trattorias, and a whole range of excellent bookshops.

Enge verwinkelte Gassen, Kopfsteinpflaster und ockerfarben getünchte Häuser schaffen ein Ambiente, das vor allem Kreative anzieht. Schon früher ein Bohemeviertel, hat sich der Stadtteil jenseits des Tibers – nichts anderes heißt Trastevere – längst als hippes Szeneviertel etabliert. Angesagte kleine Läden, Cafés, Trattorias und eine Reihe exzellente Buchläden sind hier zu entdecken.

Ses ruelles tortueuses et étroites, ses pavés et ses maisons de couleur ocre fascinent surtout les artistes. De longue date un quartier bohème, le Trastevere, situé de l'autre côté du Tibre – d'où son nom – est connu depuis longtemps comme quartier branché. Des petites boutiques tendance, des cafés, des trattorias et d'excellentes librairies attendent la découverte.

Viuzze strette e tortuose, acciottolato e case intonacate in ocra creano un ambiente che richiama soprattutto i creativi. In passato quartiere bohémien, il rione che sorge dall'altra parte del Tevere si è ormai affermato come zona di tendenza. Qui è possibile scoprire piccoli negozi, caffè e trattorie alla moda nonché una serie di librerie di prim'ordine.

Trevi Fountain

Piazza di Trevi
00187 Rome
Centro Storico

Public transportation: Bus Piazza San Silvestro
Map: No. 43

Who does not remember the image of Anita Ekberg bathing in the Trevi fountain in Fellini's film "La Dolce Vita"? These days it is strictly prohibited to set foot in the baroque structure and constantly patrolling carabinieri make sure that the rules are adhered to. It is, however, allowed to toss coins into the fountain, but only when not facing it and over one's shoulder. Apparently, this guarantees that you will return.

Die im Trevi-Brunnen badende Anita Ekberg aus Fellinis Film „La Dolce Vita" hat sich unauslöschbar ins kollektive Gedächtnis eingebrannt. Das Baden in dem barocken Prachtbrunnen ist heute strengstens verboten. Für die Einhaltung sorgen ständig patrouillierende Carabinieri. Erlaubt ist weiterhin Münzen zu werfen, aber bitte mit dem Rücken zum Wasser und über die Schulter. Das garantiert, dass man wieder kommen wird.

L'image d'Anita Ekberg se baignant dans la fontaine de Trévi dans le film de Fellini « La Dolce Vita » est gravée à jamais dans la mémoire collective. Aujourd'hui, la baignade dans cette somptueuse fontaine baroque est strictement interdite. Et les carabinieri y veillent en permanence. Il est tout de même permis d'y lancer une pièce monnaie, mais la coutume veut que ce soit par-dessus l'épaule et en tournant le dos à la fontaine. Ceci pour s'assurer de revenir à Rome !

Anita Ekberg che fa il bagno nella Fontana di Trevi nella «Dolce vita» di Fellini è un'immagine entrata a fare parte dell'immaginario collettivo. Oggi fare il bagno in questa splendida fontana è severamente proibito e i carabinieri sempre di pattuglia provvedono al rispetto di questo divieto. È invece ancora permesso gettare delle monete, ma si faccia ben attenzione a dare le spalle all'acqua mentre si lanciano: infatti, secondo la tradizione, ciò assicura che si ritornerà.

ARRIVING IN ROME

By Plane

Rome has two international airports within easy reach of the city center.
Information: Tel. +39 / 06 / 6 59 51,
www.adr.it

Aeroporto Leonardo da Vinci di Fiumicino (FCO)

Approx. 32 km/20 miles to the west of the city center. Scheduled and charter flights.

The Leonardo-Express leaves for the main railway station, the Stazione Termini, every 30 min, travel time c. 30 min. The regional service FM1 leaves every 15 min (every 30 min on Sun) for Tiburtina Station, travel time 45 min. www.trenitalia.com

There is also the bus shuttle (www.terravision.it for example), travel time 70 min. Taxi to the main station takes 45 min, between €40-60

Aeroporto Roma Ciampino (CIA)

Some 15 km/9 miles to the south east of the city center. The former military airport serves charter and budget flights.

Cotral-Busses leave every 40 min via the Ciampino Station for Anagnina metro station, travel time 15 min. Then take metro line A to the Stazione Termini. There is also a shuttle service by budget operators between the airport and the main station, Termini (www.terravision.it for example), travel time 30 min, €8. A taxi to Stazione Termini takes 35 min, approx. €30.

By Rail

There are a number of international railway services from Switzerland, Austria, Germany, France, Spain, Croatia, Slovenia, Prague, or Budapest.

Rome boasts six railway stations: Roma Tiburtina, Roma Ostiense, Roma Tuscolana, Roma Trastevere, Roma San Pietro, and the main station Roma Termini.

Further Information:

Trenitalia, Tel. +39 / 89 20 21 (0.54 €/min.), www.trenitalia.it
Stazione Termini, Tel. +39 / 06 / 4 88 17 26, www.romatermini.it

Entry and Customs Requirements

European citizens require a valid identity card. There are practically no custom limits for members of the EU. Aged 17 and over you can, for example, import 800 cigarettes, 400 cigarillos, 200 cigars, 1 kg tobacco, 10l spirits, 90l wine and 110l beer for private use.

INFORMATION

Tourist Information

APT Roma – Azienda di Promozione Turistica

Via Parigi 5
00185 Roma
Tel. +39 / 06 / 48 89 91
Fax +39 / 06 / 4 81 93 16
info@aptroma.com
www.romaturismo.com
Mon–Sat 9.30 am to 7 pm
Sub-office in Leonardo da Vinci airport, terminal B, daily 8.15 am to 7 pm.
Numerous information stands P. I. T. dotted around the city incl. the Stazione Termini, Via Nazionale, Piazza Navona, Castel Sant'Angelo.

Event Guides

You will find the monthly event guides **Un Ospite a Roma and L'Evento,** with a brief overview in English, in hotels and information centers. The weekly magazines **Roma c'è** and the English-language **Time Out Roma** as well as the Thursday supplement **Trovaroma** of the Roman daily paper "La Repubblica" contain information on events, restaurants, bars, and leisure activities.

Websites
General
www.romaturismo.com – the Roman tourism information portal with comprehensive accommodation guide and well-arranged event calendar (Ital., En.)
www.comune.roma.it – the city council's official website (Ital.)
www.vatican.va – official Vatican portal, incl. information on the liturgical year as well as the Vatican's museums and libraries (Ital., En., Span., Fr., Ger., Port., Chin., Latin)

Going Out
www.timeout.com/rome – Restaurants and bars, shopping, night life, event guide (En.)
www.2night.it (Ital., En.)

The Arts & Culture
www.beniculturali.it – ministry of culture's website with links to the main museums and archaeological sites (Ital.)
www.museiincomuneroma.it – official portal of the Roman museums (Ital., En., Span., Fr.)
www.museionline.it – museums, exhibitions, and excavations all over Italy (Ital.)
www.auditorium.com – the modern concert hall's portal incl. program (Ital., En., Fr.)
www.spettacoloromano.it – contains the program of some 50 theaters in and around Rome (Ital., En.)

Sport & Leisure
www.parcoappiaantica.org – all you need to know about the regional park Appia Antica (Ital., En.)
www.termediroma.org – Tivoli spa (Ital., En.)
www.villaborghese.it – leisure facilities in the park of the Villa Borghese (Ital., En.)

Street-Map
www.maps.google.it – interactive street map (En., Ger.)

Accommodation
www.alberghi.romaturismo.it – list of accommodation by the Roman tourist board incl. web-links (Ital., En.)
www.bbitalia.it – bed & breakfast in the whole of Italy incl. Rome (Ital., En., Span., Fr., Ger.)
www.romeby.com – hotels, guesthouses, and rooms, vacation rental (Ital., En., Span., Fr., Ger.)
www.romaclick.com – hotels, bed & breakfast, vacation rental (Ital., En., Span., Fr., Ger.)

Entertainment Guide
www.romeguide.it – contains an entertainment guide and ticket sales (Ital., En., Ger.)
www.gorome.it – contains an entertainment guide (Ital., En.)

FURTHER LITERATURE

Charles Richard
The New Italians von 1994: A refreshing account of modern-day life in Italy.

Johann Wolfgang von Goethe
Italian Journey. During his travels to Italy from November 1786 to April 1788, Goethe lived for more than one year, including breaks, in the Via del Corso 18 in Rome.

Wolfgang Koeppen
Death in Rome. A family reunion in Rome after World War II. Former Wehrmacht general Judejahn wants to return to Germany. The national socialist reign of terror catches up with victims, perpetrators, and following

generations alike in the city of Caesar and Mussolini.

Alberto Moravia

The Woman of Rome. Life confessions of the beautiful street prostitute Adriana, who grows up in the Rome of the 1920s. The film version with Gina Lollobrigida and the Catholic Church's indignation helped the book to cult status.

Peter Prange

La Principessa. Rome 1623. The two ingenious baroque architects Lorenzo Bernini and Francesco Borromini fight tooth and nail for the favor of the young and beautiful Clarissa from England, as well as for contracts, reputation, and fame.

Robert Graves

I, Claudius. The amusing yet enthralling biography of the Roman emperor counts as the prototype of the historical novel.

SIGHTSEEING

City Tours
Bus and Streetcar

Public transport is ideal for reasonably priced city tours. The **electro bus lines 116, 117, and 119** are recommended for exploring the old part of town, although they are pretty crowded. The **expressline 64 and bus line 64** operate between the Vatican and the Stazione Termini and the **bus line 170** between Termini and Trastevere. **Streetcar line 3** from Trastevere to the Villa Borghese is well worth a ride.

Sightseeing Buses

The Roman public transport (ATAC) offers two bus sightseeing tours. During the day, the open red double decker buses of **line 110open** operate a high frequency service between 80 places of interest. The hop-on-hop-off system includes ten stops, commentary in Italian and English, duration approx. 2 hours, a ticket for the day costs €13. The 16 seater **Archeobus** leaves the central railway station every hour to tour the antique center to the Via Appia Antica. Possibility to alight at any of 14 stops, commentary in Italian and English, duration 1 ¾ hours, a ticket for the day costs €8. Combined ticket for both tours €20. Information: Tel. +39 / 8 00 28 12 81, www.trambusopen.com

In addition you will find a number of private companies offering **city and special tours** with **commentary**. Duration approx. 2 hours, tickets from €30 as well as **round trips** with the possibility of a break, tickets €19. A selection of operators:

Appian Line, Piazza dell'Esquilino 6/7, Tel. +39 / 06 / 48 78 66 01, www.appianline.it
Carrani Viaggi, Via Vittorio Emanuele Orlando 95, Tel +39 / 06 / 4 74 25 01, www.carrani.com
Green Line Tours, Via Giovanni Amendola, 32, Tel. +39 / 06 / 4 82 74 80 www.greenlinetours.com

Boat Trips
Batelli di Roma

Tel. +39 / 06 / 97 74 54 98, www.battellidiroma.it
For some years, the city has been trying to develop the River Tiber for tourism with boat trips and evening events. However, in some places the quay walls are so high that you cannot see the city. There is a **regular boat service** between the Isola Tiberina/Calata Aguillara and the Ponte Duca d'Aosta, a single ticket costs between €1-3. There are four **round trips with commentary** starting from the Ponte Duca d'Aosta leaving at 11 am, 12.30 am, 4 pm and 5.30 pm, duration approx. 1 ¼ hrs. Breaks are possible, tickets €12. There is also a **Diner's Cruise** available in the evenings, departure at 9 pm, duration 2 ¼ hrs., tickets €54. The day trip from the Ponte Marconi to the antique port of Ostia Antica is well worth it, departure 9.30 am, tickets €13.

Bicycle Tours

The extensive park of the Villa Borghese is ideal for a bike tour. The Via Appia Antica is just as appealing on Sundays, when it is closed to cars. A mountain bike is best suited to the up to 20 km/12 mile long bumpy ride. Bike hire:

Bici Pincio, Viale de Villa Medici (Villa Borghese), Tel. +39 / 06 / 6 78 43 74

Via Appia Antica 58/60, Tel. +39 / 06 / 5 13 53 16, Mon–Sat 9.30 am – 5.30 pm or 4.30 pm during the winter months, www.parcoappiaantica.org.

Guided City Tours
Enjoy Rome

Via Marghera 8a
Tel. +39 / 06 / 44 51 84 3
www.enjoyrome.com
Guided city tour in English with a number of focal points such as antique Rome, the former Jewish Ghetto, the catacombs, or Rome at night, duration 3 hours, from €22 (up to age 26) and from €27 (26 and above).

RomaCulta

Tel. +39 / 33 87 60 74 70
www.romaculta.it
Individual city tour and cultural guided walks. Reservation required.

Overlooks
Monumento Nazionale a Vittorio Emanuele II

The terrace of this 70m/230 ft tall monument proffers a panoramic view over the ancient city and the rooftops of the old part of town.

St. Peter

The ascent into the 120m/393 ft tall dome will be rewarded with a sublime view of the inside of St. Peter and a breathtaking panorama of Rome. You should not be afraid of heights or confined spaces.

Piazzale Garibaldi

Standing on the Gianicolo hill on a clear day, you can see the Alban Hills and the Appennine Mountains with the River Tiber, the Castel Sant'Angelo, the dome of the Pantheon, and the Monumento Nazionale a Vittorio Emanuele II at your feet. Especially striking after nightfall.

Aerophile Italia

www.aerophile.com
The ascent in the securely tethered hot-air balloon near the racecourse of the Villa Borghese provides both a breathtaking view and quite a thrill. Daily March – Oct., €15–18 per person.

TICKETS & REDUCTIONS

Ticket Offices
Hellò Ticket

Tel. +39 / 06 / 48 07 84 00
www.helloticket.it
Box office: Orbis Servizi, Piazza Esquilino 37

Ticketeria

Tel. +39 / 06 / 3 28 10
Fax +39 / 06 / 32 65 13 29
www.ticketeria.it
Ticket service for a number of Roman museums, some of which require advance notification.

Reductions
Roma Pass

Free public transport and free entry to two museums as well as reduced prices for many other museums and events. Available from the Roman tourist board, museums, and online under www.ticketclic.it, 3 day pass €20, www.romapass.it

Museum Pass

Three strip tickets reduce entry to museums and other places of interest. They are valid for seven days and available from the Roman tourist board, museums, or online from www.ticketclic.it

Roma Archeologica Card (Colosseo, Palatino, Palazzo Massimo, Palazzo Altemps, Crypta Balbi, Terme di Diocleziano, Terme di Caracalla, Tomba di Cecilia Metella, Villa dei Quintili), €23.50

Capitolini Card (Musei Capitolini, Centrale Montemartini), €9

Appia Antica Card (Terme di Caracalla, Tomba di Cecilia Metella, Villa dei Quintili), €7.50

GETTING AROUND IN ROME

Public Transport
ATAC

Tel. +39 / 06 / 5 70 03, www.atac.roma.it
The quickest way of getting around are the two subway lines A and B. The metro runs Mon-Fri from 5.30 am to 11.30 pm during the week and until 1.30 am at weekends. After that, night buses 55 N and 40 N run throughout the night. The most important intra-urban means of transport are buses and streetcars. Between 1.30 am and 5.30 am there are 22 night buses (N) which run every 30 min. Express buses (X) only stop at every second or third stop. Tickets (biglietti) are available from ticket machines in metro stations (change only for coins up to €2), kiosks, most bars, tobacco shops (tabacchi), and supermarkets.

A single ticket (BIT) for €1 is valid for 75 min after validation. A five-strip ticket can be used over a number of days. For unlimited travel, purchase a day ticket for €4 (BIG), a three-day ticket for €11 (BTI), a seven-day ticket for €16 (CIS), or the Roma Pass (see above).

Network plans and timetables are available from the ATAC website as downloads or to be used interactively.

Taxi

Samarcanda, Tel. +39 / 06 / 55 51
La Capitale, Tel. +39 / 06 / 49 94
Surcharges apply for night journeys or during Sunday, for transporting large items of baggage, or for many people. Only use licensed taxis (identification number on doors, boot, and inside)! Taxis are white or yellow and all have a taximeter.

Central Taxi Phone Number: +39 / 1 99 60 11 06
(5 to 18 cent per minute, depending on the time of day)

Scooter and Vespa

These powered two-wheelers are the Romans' favorite means of transport. Those wishing to emulate them beware—it is not easy to cope with the chaotic traffic conditions and cars come perilously close. Rental starts at €35 per day incl. insurance, helmet, and lock.

Bike e Scooter Rental, Via Cavour 80,
Tel. +39 / 06 / 4 81 56 69, www.scooterhire.it, open: 9 am to 7 pm.

www.ecomoverent.com (bicycles, scooters, and motorbikes), Via Varese 48-50,
Tel. +39 / 06 / 44 70 45 18, daily 8.30 am to 7.30 pm.

EVENTS

Befana
January 5/6, the witch Befana rides on her broom from house to house to present well-behaved children with a sock full of sweets. Epiphany market with lots of gift articles and souvenirs on the Piazza Navona.

Festa delle Donne
March 8, International Women's Day incl. demonstrations and rallies.

Festa di San Giuseppe
March 19, festive day in honor of St. Joseph and Italian father's day. Bakeries serve traditional bignè di San Giuseppe (filled cream puffs) and fritelle (crullers). The Trionfale neighborhood is well known for its folksy festival.

Maratona
Middle of March, city marathon (www.maratonadi-roma.it).

Festa delle Palme
Sunday before Easter, festive sanctification of olive branches on St. Peter's Square.

Pasqua
Easter, Holy Thursday: the Maundy in the Basilica of St. John Lateran; midnight papal mass on Good Friday on Palatine Hill and the cross procession at the Colosseum; papal blessing "Urbi et Orbi" at noon on Easter Sunday on St. Peter's square.

Natale di Roma
April 20/21, festival on the Capitoline Hill on the occasion of the founding of Rome with flag tossers, bands, and fireworks (www.gsr-roma.com).

Festa del Lavoro
May 1, Labor Day, free pop concert on the Piazza San Giovanni with national and international stars.

Concorso Ippico Internazionale
End of May, international equestrian festival with formation riding by the Carabinieri on the Piazza di Siena in the park of the Villa Borghese.

Estate Romana
Middle of June to Middle of Sept., Roman cultural summer with a plethora of events (www.estateromana.comune.roma.it).

San Giovanni
June 23/24, public festival to celebrate John the Apostle near the Basilica of St. John Lateran with culinary delicacies, dancing, music, and fireworks

San Pietro e Paolo
June 29, celebratory papal mass in St. Peter's Basilica to honor St. Peter.

Trevere Expò
July, booths selling arts and crafts and culinary tidbits from the Roman provinces on the shore of the River Tiber.

L'Isola del Cinema
June–Sept., open-air cinema on Tiber Island (www.isoladelcinema.com).

Festa de' Noantri
Second half of July, two-week folk festival in Trastevere with procession, folk dancing, and songs, culinary delicacies, fireworks.

Madonna della Neve
August 5, lavish light show and deployment of snow

canons in remembrance of the wondrous creation of the church Santa Maria Maggiore.

Festa Internazionale di Roma

Middle of October, international film festival (www.romacinemafest.org).

Natale

Middle of December–January 6, Christmas market on the Piazza Navona, nativity scenes in numerous churches, midnight mass in St. Peter's Basilica on 24, papal blessing "Urbi et Orbi" on St. Peter's Square at noon on Christmas Day.

Veglia di Capodanno

New Year's Eve, public concerts on the Piazza del Popolo, Quirinale, and St. Peter's Square (www.capodanno.roma.it).

IMPORTANT INFORMATION

Money

Currency: Euro (€)
Debit and Credit Cards: Maestro or credit cards can be used to obtain money from ATMs or used as a method of payment in most hotels, restaurants, and shops.

EMERGENCY

Police: Tel. 113
Caribinieri: Tel. 112
Ambulance: Tel. 118
Fire Department: Tel. 115

Business Hours

Banks: Mon–Fri 8.30 am to 1.30 pm, 2.30/3 pm to 3.30/4.30 pm, some banks open Tue–Sat.
Shops: Mon–Sat 9/10 am to 1/2 pm, 4 pm to 8 pm, sometimes even during lunchtime, evenings until 10 pm and Sundays. Grocery shops are closed on Thu pm during the winter months, all other shops Mon am. During the summer all shops are closed Sat pm. August is a favorite month for the vacation close-down.
Museums: Usually 9/10 am to 6/7 pm. Small outfits often close pm. Most are closed on Mon.
Restaurants: Lunch approx. 12.30 am to 2.30 pm, dinner approx. 7.30 pm to 10.30 pm. Most close on Sun., vacation close-down primarily in August.

Prices

Accommodation in a simple hotel for two people in a twin room (incl. breakfast) from €80. A multi-course dinner in a Trattoria weighs in at €25-40 per person incl. house wine. Prices for a café latte, a soft drink, or a beer hover around €3 at the bar or between €5-6 when ordered outside on the terrace.

Smoking

Smoking is prohibited in all public spaces incl. airports, train stations, buses, streetcars, restaurants, and bars. Larger restaurants may boast separate rooms for smokers.

Tourist Seasons

The best time to visit Rome is between the end of April and beginning of July or between the middle of September and the end of October. During vacations and around Easter and Pentecost, the city is inundated with tour groups. Most Romans are on holiday from Ferragosto (August 15), when the city is empty and many restaurants and shops are closed. Temperatures can reach 40°C/104°F. It seldom falls below zero °C/32°F in the winter. There is a lot of rain in November and December and the icy Tramontana wind hits Rome in January.

Security

The crime rate in Rome is pretty much comparable to those of other large European cities. Don't venture around the main railway station, the Piazza Vittorio Emanuele II, and the Piazza Albania as well as parks (such as the Villa Borghese) at night. Skillful pickpockets incl. gangs of begging children feel at home in overcrowded public transportation.

Telephone

Area Code Rome: The area code in Italy is part of the normal number and has to be dialed at all times.
Calling from Abroad: +39 plus telephone number (incl. first zero!)
Calling from Rome: Country code plus telephone number (incl. first zero!)
Directory Assistance: Tel. 412
Online Telephone Directory: www.paginebianche.it

Public telephones require calling cards (scheda telefonica), which can be obtained in tobacco shops (tabacchi), kiosks, and some bars. Tear off the perforated corner before use.

Tips

Prices usually include service (servizio). Those satisfied with the service in a restaurant, hotel, or taxi add a tip. Restaurants almost always have a cover charge (pane e coperto) of approx. €1.50–3.00 per person.

Internet Cafés

Easy Everything, Via Barberini 2, www.easyinternetcafe.com
Internet Café, Via dei Marrucini 12, www.internetcafe.it
Internet Train, Via Cardinale Merry Del Val 20, www.internettrain.it
TreviNet Pl@ce, Via in Arcione103 (Fontana di Trevi)
Visit **www.romawireless.com** to find wireless hot spots in Rome.

Via Giulio Cesare

Via Cola di Rienz

Città del Vaticano

TIBER

Via Gregorio VII

Corso Vittori Emanuele

Gianicolo

Via Vitellia

Villa Borghese

Piazza del Popolo

Corso d'Italia

Piazza di Spagna

Via del Tritone

Stazione Termini

Via del Corso

Via Nazionale

Via dei Fori Imperiali

Parco di Traiano

Isola Tiberina

Lungotevere Aventino

Viale di Trastevere

Parco Ninfeo di Nerone

Other titles by teNeues

ISBN 978-3-8327-9309-8

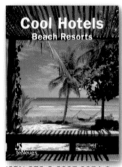

ISBN 978-3-8327-9274-9

ISBN 978-3-8327-9237-4

ISBN 978-3-8327-9247-3

ISBN 978-3-8327-9234-3

ISBN 978-3-8327-9308-1

ISBN 978-3-8327-9243-5

ISBN 978-3-8327-9230-5

ISBN 978-3-8327-9248-0

Size: **15 x 19 cm**, 6 x 7½ in., 224 pp., **Flexicover**, c. 200 color photographs,
Text: English / German / French / Spanish / Italian
www.teneues.com

Other titles by teNeues

ISBN 978-3-8327-9342-5

ISBN 978-3-8327-9343-2

ISBN 978-3-8327-9296-1

ISBN 978-3-8327-9293-0

ISBN 978-3-8327-9294-7

ISBN 978-3-8327-9295-4

Interior Pages
Cool Guide New York

Size: **15 x 19 cm**, 6 x 7 ½ in., 224 pp., **Flexicover**, c. 250 color photographs,
Text: English / German / French / Spanish
www.teneues.com

On a divine mission: after his second official visit to Germany in 2006, Pope Benedict XVI flew home once again on the "Regensburg."

The Eternal City

Rome, the city built on seven hills, was founded, as legend tells us, more than 2,700 years ago by Romulus. Since then, the capital of the Roman Empire has flourished and expanded its confines. Today, the Eternal City sprawls over an area of close to 500 square miles, vastly greater than the 0.17 square miles occupied by the smallest country in the world: Vatican City. Though only a fraction of the size of Rome, the immense influence of the Vatican has taken its papal heads of state on journeys around the globe. In the past thirty years, Pope Benedict XVI and his predecessor Pope John Paul II have visited Germany five times, always relying on the services of Lufthansa. Our Airbus A321, named "Regensburg," sports a plaque with the papal coat of arms commemorating Pope Benedict's flight home on the aircraft from the 20th World Youth Day staged in Cologne in August 2005. Equally welcome aboard Lufthansa's flights to Rome are passengers making a personal visit to Vatican City, St. Peter's Square and the Basilica.

Lufthansa flies there – several times daily and at very attractive fares. View all the details about our flights to Rome and others to more than 200 destinations around the world at www.lufthansa.com. There's no better way to fly.

A STAR ALLIANCE MEMBER